ENDORSEM

The man is the message. If ever this were true, it would be true of Leif Hetland and *The Love Awakening*. I've had the unusual privilege of watching the formation of both. And yet calling it a privilege is an awkward understatement, as it feels like I was given a backstage pass to the greatest show on earth— the transformational love of God on display in and through one surrendered person: my friend Leif Hetland. I've seen it first-hand in the pulpit, watched the impact of the man and the message all over the world, and even tasted of it in my home as we fellowshipped together. And I'm excited to say, I now see it in print. This book that you now hold in your hands has the potential to impart to each reader the lens through which Jesus sees the world, the lens called the Father's love. Seeing everything through His love changes life as we know it! The brilliant insights, the moving stories, and the humility with which this writer writes are sure to draw you, the reader, into your own transformational journey with the Father's love.

Bill Johnson

Pastor, Bethel Church, Redding, California

Author of *The Way of Life* and *Born for Significance*

Leif writes with warmth about the seeds of Heaven's Kingdom, each one planted in a human heart so that we might grow up into the *"fullness of Christ"* (Ephesians. 4:13). To nurture this promise in ourselves is to be compelled by love—to labor with joy, to bear fruit, to give ourselves away so that the grace lavished on us may multiply into the life of God's family on earth. For many years we have honored Leif for his wisdom, compassion, and great courage in bringing the Gospel to places where discipleship may come at extraordinary cost. Where he has witnessed suffering, we have mourned with him, as he has surely mourned with us. But all the more we share an overwhelming hope and comfort beyond words. Let his book shine a bright light on that hope, the harvest for which we are called together, the renewal of creation springing forth from the same everlasting love that God bears for you here and now, yesterday and forever.

HEIDI G. BAKER, PhD
Co-founder and President, Iris Global

Leif Hetland's new book, *The Love Awakening*, roots the believer, whether new or established, in an important foundational truth: the love of God experienced in our lives. I agree strongly with the need for a baptism of love. When I pray for people to be filled with the Holy Spirit, I pray for them to be baptized both in power and in love. Leif has taught in my schools of healing and impartation for many years where he has brought this message of love in powerful ways. He is an excellent communicator. Leif is called the ambassador of love in his work with Muslims in Middle Eastern countries. His insights into the ministry of love and the importance of looking up to God, looking inside our hearts, and looking out to the world are solid discipleship principles. I love his amazing stories that illustrate his teaching on love. Buy and read *The Love Awakening* and have any possible love deficits met as you gain faith to receive more of the love of God.

—RANDY CLARK, DD, DMIN, ThD, MDIV, BS
Overseer of the Apostolic Network of Global Awakening
President of Global Awakening Theological Seminary

I couldn't be more excited about a book than I am this one. When was the last time you read a book on love? Why are there so few books on love? The greatest deficiency in our faith today is between how we live and love and the greatest commandment. Thank you, Leif, for writing this.

Please read this book slowly and reflectively. Be baptized in love and love radically.

Bob Roberts
Founder, GlocalNet and Northwood Church
Author

Leif's insights and teachings are a tremendous gift to the Body of Christ. Two of his previous books, *Healing the Orphan Spirit* and *Called to Reign*, have delivered to me some of the most impactful teachings that have changed the way I lead myself and others. In his latest book, *The Love Awakening: Living Immersed in the Supernatural Love of God*, he continues to unfold the answers to living a life of *sonship/daughtership* through a baptism of God's love. If you are reading this endorsement, please do not wait any longer to open this book and dive into the rich truth you will find in it. I know it will impact you the way that it has impacted me.

Dr. Jon Chasteen
President, The King's University and Seminary
Lead Pastor, Victory Church, Oklahoma City, Oklahoma

Jesus taught that there were two great commandments and they had one thing in common: LOVE! This is the vital and core message of the Gospel. Paul taught in First Corinthians 13 that if we don't have love, we have nothing, we are nothing, and it profits nothing, outlining that love is the foundation for all we are and do in our journey of faith. Leif Hetland is a true ambassador of love who has transformed people, tribes, and nations by walking in this one Kingdom mandate. *The Love Awakening* will call you to join God's company of love ambassadors. This is a must-read and a book that should be on every believer's bookshelf.

PATRICIA KING
Author, Minister, Media Producer and Host

This book contains the core message of my friend Leif Hetland, known around the world as the ambassador (or apostle) of love! His profound insights are conveyed in simple language with powerful stories and illustrations that have the potential to radically transform individuals and communities. I highly recommend this book!

DR. JOSEPH MATTERA
National Convener of the United States
Coalition of Apostolic Leaders

Love is more than our duty; it is our destiny! Leif Hetland has given us such incredible insights into God's love and how it shapes us and forms our true identity before the Father. You will enjoy reading firsthand accounts of how God's love has rocked the nations of the earth. Leif is truly the ambassador of love. I know no one more qualified to write *The Love Awakening: Living Immersed in the Supernatural Love of God!* As you read this book, you will *feel* the very Love who stepped out of eternity step into your heart. It will change you and awaken you! The love of God will cascade over your thirsty soul as you read each chapter.

Be sure to get *two* copies of this book, one for yourself and one for a friend. Believe me, they will thank you for it!

BRIAN SIMMONS
Passion & Fire Ministries

The Love Awakening is a journey into the transformative, supernatural love of God. Leif's experiential immersion in Abba's love has profoundly impacted our lives and the lives of countless others around the world. You will be deeply stirred by this timely message as your course is shifted directly into Love Himself!

ALBERTO and KIMBERLY RIVERA

I have known Leif for more than twenty years; I have worked with him and observed his ever-increasing desire to walk in the Kingdom of God and model agape love in every aspect of his life. If anyone can write about living immersed in the supernatural love of God, it's Leif Hetland. I highly recommend reading this book to receive your own personal insights into the depths of God's love. Be prepared to be Kingdom inspired, informed, challenged, and blessed!

FRIEDE TAYLOR
Author of *From Hitler's Germany to the Cross of Christ and Beyond*

I have the deepest regard for Leif Hetland. He lives what he preaches, and he exudes the triune life as he walks in the love of the triune God. His heart of compassion has moved me time and again to realize there are no dark places in our souls or on the planet that love cannot reach. I am persuaded that in this hour we need to cultivate afresh our contemplation of the love of the triune God as revealed in the Lord Jesus Christ. *The Love Awakening* can help us to embrace the divine dance of love and share that love with the whole world. Thanks, Leif, for your faithfulness and transparency.

Dr. Mark J. Chironna
Church On The Living Edge
Mark Chironna Ministries

Leif Hetland is one of the most courageous, fiery lovers of God that I've ever met. His extraordinary stories will awaken your heart to burn with that same fiery love as you encounter the God of love Himself, empowering you to love your world and transform it with intense supernatural love.

Duncan Smith
President, Catch The Fire

Leif has such a deep revelation of love, and I know that his revelation is not superficial because I have seen, even in my own life, how much his gift of love has the power to awaken a soul during difficult times. There are so many things that touched me in this heartfelt love letter to Papa God and Leif's fellow man, but this one quote stood out for me personally: "People who are not well acquainted with supernatural love may be more ready than they have ever been for demonstrations of it," and then he talks about the uselessness of unkind debates, personal doctrine, and our ineffectiveness to create environments that attract these hungry people. "But they are moved by our love when we carry it authentically within us." Such profound words and revelation. I pray that millions get to experience this cultural reformative book because love is really the only way to accurately reveal Jesus.

Leon Schoeman
President, ORI International

In *The Love Awakening* Leif Hetland uncorks a revelatory, prophetic fountain of the great deep lending profound, experiential insight to the breadth, length, height, and depth of love. This *person* of love is relentlessly intimate, sacrificial, preeminent, and accessible. In a day when the word has prophesied that the "love of many will grow cold" (Matthew 24:12), Leif flips this narrative and personifies this consuming fire of love every soul is longing for. This book is a clarion call and a must-read for all believers everywhere.

SCOTT WILLIAM WINTERS
Actor, Producer

Leif Hetland's book *The Love Awakening* is an invitation from the heart of the Father for all of us to experience richer relationship with Him. God is love, and His heart for each of us to be filled with a continual overflow of His Spirit and nature is so powerfully explained through Leif's sharing of his journey into a revelation of sonship and encounter with the Father's love. Leif lives so authentically as an ambassador of love, and in this book he shares the keys that he has found to breaking through into living practically in this love that the Father wants us all to experience. Christ in us and us in Him is the place of continuous strength and joy, and this book will truly help you in learning how to live "immersed in the supernatural love of God."

KATHERINE RUONALA
Senior Leader, Glory City Church

Leif's personal walk has always been an outward demonstration for me of how to embrace and walk in the Father's love. The essence of Leif's message is so grounded and saturated in the truth of who He is, your perspectives will, without a doubt, be challenged and transformed. As Leif shares accounts of his own authentic journey, his message urges us to strip away the things that demand our attention in order to realize our true identity through the revelation of God's supernatural love. My own heart breaks at the thought of our younger generations not encountering this deep love and revelation of Jesus. The tangible genuineness of *The Love Awakening* will renew mindsets and restore generations.

STEVE ROBERTSON
CEO, BOLD-Education

Leif Hetland's newest offering is more than a book; it is a love reformation road map for sons and daughters. Get ready for a fresh baptism in the divine love of God and be empowered to walk in the fullness of the supernatural power that Christ so dearly paid for us to have.

GEORGIAN BANOV
Co-founder, Global Celebration and
GCSSM Online School
Author of *Joy! God's Secret Weapon for Every Believer*

No one is better suited to write on the love of God than Papa Leif. My first encounter with the man the world calls the apostle of love left me sobbing as my broken orphaned heart was suddenly filled with the Father's love. Papa Leif was simply releasing what he carries—a God love so strong and reassuring that my poor thirsty soul was immediately saturated like a dry sponge drenched in water. Immediately things began to change. I had been in a season of elongated fierce warfare and was battle weary and worn. But suddenly I had a peace that came in the form of Papa God's total reassurance and protection. The enemy backed off in the presence of an all-powerful Papa who truly cares for His children. The lie that God had abandoned me was broken, and the truth of His love enveloped me like a warm blanket. It was life changing. In his book *The Love Awakening*, Papa Leif says this same encounter is coming to the world, first as a trickle, then a flow, then an immersion. I want it! The world needs it! Let us all get positioned to receive it.

KATIE SOUZA
Katie Souza Ministries

This is truly Leif Hetland's life message. With so many voices out there talking about secondary issues, Leif focuses on the core message of Jesus. God wove the thread of His love throughout history, from Eden to the cross. And through the Holy Spirit, He will continue to be Love in the flesh through you and me. This book will give you a picture of what love is. Prepare your heart to grow in your understanding of being fully loved and be ready to represent love.

WILL HART
CEO, Iris Global

More than ever we need a love revolution in our society. Many have written about this vital and important subject of love, but so few have written with divine revelation. Thank you to my friend Leif Hetland for sharing with us, without restraint, the deep studies with strong revelations he received that are more powerful than a bomb. My two favorite people who have written and demonstrated true love are Mother Teresa and my spiritual mother Dr. Heidi Baker. But today I am so grateful to hear the voice of a man, in the true sense of the word, to write about this subject in a way that is not "pinky honeyed" but manly and even with poetry (being of French-speaking Swiss origin and therefore sensitive to the expression of love). *The Love Awakening* is a treasure full of keys to revolutionize our daily life.

JEAN-LUC TRACHSEL
Founder, Jean-Luc Trachsel Ministries
President, International Association of Healing Ministries

In *The Love Awakening: Living Immersed in the Supernatural Love of God*, Leif Hetland shares with us what he knows best: the Father's heart. What I love most about this book is how Leif emphasizes how important it is for us to receive the deep yet simple revelation of our union with God *before* we are launched out into our destinies. Far too many Christians dedicate their lives to *live for Christ* without discovering the revelation of their *oneness* with Christ that eventually reveals the mysterious divine exchange of our lives dying while Christ lives His life through us to accomplish His purposes on the earth. *Love Awakening* is an incredibly important message to this strange and broken world we are living in, and I thank God for my friend Leif Hetland and for his unrelenting pursuit to discover the treasures and secrets hidden deep inside God's heart.

BRIAN "HEAD" WELCH
Co-founder of the Grammy Award–winning band Korn
New York Times best-selling author
of *Save Me from Myself*
Costar of *Loud Krazy Love*

The Love Awakening by my friend Leif Hetland provides a beautiful and vulnerable reminder that each of us is created to be loved supernaturally—to live from love, rather than for love. As cofounder of Global Mission Awareness and the Kingdom Family Movement, Leif knows from personal experience that when our orphaned hearts are transformed by the Father's love, we are adopted in our new identity as sons and daughters into the family of God's love. In these pages, the author encourages, equips, and empowers readers to join a new reformation of God's love as His ambassadors that will reveal His heart to the world. I encourage you to join him in this great adventure.

LARRY ROSS
Founder and CEO, A. Larry Ross Communications

What I love about *The Love Awakening* and all Leif Hetland's writing is that he immediately takes me beyond the surface and into a zone of miraculous revelation. I am awed by that quality. What I learned was more than what I was reading. When our minds are so impacted, it makes the message a permanent part of our memory bank. Thank you, Leif, for such enrichment! I am forever blessed and honored to be a spiritual father and mentor in your life! I eagerly recommend *The Love Awakening.*

CHARLES CARRIN, DD
Spiritual Father and Mentor to the Author
Founder, Charles Carrin Ministries
Author of *Spirit-Empowered Theology*
and *Hooray and Hallelujah*

THE
LOVE
AWAKENING

THE
LOVE
AWAKENING

LIVING IMMERSED IN THE
SUPERNATURAL LOVE
OF GOD

LEIF HETLAND

DESTINY IMAGE® PUBLISHERS, INC.

P.O. Box 310, Shippensburg, PA 17257-0310

"Promoting Inspired Lives."

This book and all other Destiny Image and Destiny Image Fiction books are available at Christian bookstores and distributors worldwide.

Cover design by Eileen Rockwell

Interior design by Terry Clifton

For more information on foreign distributors, call 717-532-3040.

Reach us on the Internet: www.destinyimage.com.

ISBN 13 TP: 978-0-7684-6232-6

ISBN 13 eBook: 978-0-7684-6233-3

For Worldwide Distribution, Printed in the U.S.A.

1 2 3 4 5 6 7 8 / 26 25 24 23 22

DEDICATION

I dedicate this book to my wife, best friend, ministry and covenant partner, Jennifer. *The Love Awakening* was sparked by the unwavering love you have given me for more than thirty-two years. You have taught me and challenged me to be empowered by grace and compelled by love in and out of every season of life. I am so grateful.

Forever yours,

Leif

ACKNOWLEDGMENTS

It takes a family to help an author birth a vision. I first want to honor Jesus, the core of this manuscript and the center of my life. I am so grateful to God for all the amazing people intertwined in my story. This book would not have been possible without the hard work and intentionality of several key people.

To my wife, Jennifer: Thank you for your patient and long-suffering love. You taught me the principles outlined in this book. I learned by watching you live and love every day.

To my children, Leif Emmanuel, Laila Ann, Courtney, and Katherine: I am so honored I get to be your dad. And I am so proud you are mine. Thank you for giving me the grace to receive and become this message of love so that I could release it to the world.

To my spiritual son, Paul Yadao: God knew we would need each other. Your life and leadership are priceless in every aspect of us becoming love.

To my staff at Global Mission Awareness: I want to thank my Executive Assistant, Kayleigh Dahman, for taking this book from good to great. I would also like to honor my Executive Director, David Cho, and my staff, Elise Keropian and Paule-Anne Lewis, for making me better than I am.

To Chris Tiegreen: You played a significant role in helping me take what is in my heart and communicate it on paper. It was an invaluable help.

To my spiritual family, Papa Jack Taylor and Friede Taylor: This manuscript and the stories that fill it would not have been possible without your wisdom and guidance. Papa Jack was supposed to write the foreword to this book but passed away unexpectedly on April 25, 2021. I want to honor His "yes" in the pursuit of the Kingdom of God. He was one of my most significant examples and champions of a life that lives love out loud.

To Dr. R.T. Kendall: Thank you for stepping in and writing the foreword to this book. Your friendship and wisdom over the last two decades have shaped who I am today.

To Shaun Tabatt and Destiny Image: It is an honor to be a trusted voice on your platform. Thank you for inviting me to be a part of your family.

To the global Kingdom Family Movement: You are living *The Love Awakening* in a way that inspires and gives faith, hope, and love to the world. Thank you for your ongoing sacrificial love. The world will never be the same!

CONTENTS

FOREWORD

My first memory of Leif Hetland was in a Southern Baptist Church over twenty years ago near Chattanooga, Tennessee. I was still the pastor of Westminster Chapel, visiting Chattanooga as a guest preacher. It was there that I also met Charles Carrin, a man I would team up with later on with the late Jack Taylor. Leif was part of a prayer ministry that took place between the preaching services.

What initially impressed me about Leif was his apparent gift of laying on of hands. In a word, it was extraordinary. When he prayed for my wife, Louise, she could not physically stand but fell under the power of the Spirit. I had never seen anything quite like it. Leif obviously had this gift with virtually every person he prayed for. The second thing I remember about Leif was his combination of a Norwegian and Southern accent!

Leif was born in Stavanger, Norway, in 1966. He moved to Los Angeles, California, in 1985. He married Jennifer in 1989. They have four children. He founded Global Mission Awareness in 1999. Leif received the International Peace Award from the president of Pakistan as an ambassador of love.

One morning Jack Taylor said to me during a weekend preaching at the Ada First Baptist Church in Oklahoma, "R. T., I'm going to make you rich and famous." He did not keep his promise, but he tried. We agreed to invite Charles Carrin to join us in holding Word, Spirit, and Power (WSP) conferences. Leif organized our first conference in Columbus, Georgia, in 2000. Our second WSP conference was held shortly after in Westminster Chapel. I was set up to be the "word" man, Jack the "Spirit" man, and Charles the "power" man. The three of us ended up having ninety-five WSP conferences all over America, from Florida to Alaska, New Mexico to Connecticut. Leif took my place on the team on at least three occasions when I could not be present.

I should tell you that Jack Taylor was set to write this foreword just before he died this year. I am greatly honored to be Leif's plan B, only hoping I can give due honor to both Jack and Leif.

Leif has been given an extraordinary ministry to, of all places, Pakistan. I don't know how he does it, but he risks his life in that Islamic country where he has been amazingly received. They regard him as an apostle of love. Indeed, he heard these words from the Lord while in Oslo, Norway, that he felt called to be an apostle of love. He was blessed by the power of the Spirit to such a profound sense of the love of God while still in his native country. Indeed, Leif was given such a sense of God's love that he never got over it!

The Love Awakening is a book every Christian will enjoy. It is filled with love. Leif deals coherently and helpfully with the frivolous uses of love so popular nowadays. You will read this book and sense the heart of a man from Norway who loves God, loves America, loves people, loves his wife and family, and would love you too if he met you! May this love overflow into your heart as you read on.

Dr. R.T. Kendall
Minister, Westminster Chapel, 1977–2002
Author of *We've Never Been This Way
Before* and *Total Forgiveness*

INTRODUCTION

I was speaking in a town in Norway, and it was twenty degrees below zero outside. But it's always warm where Papa God is, and He was making Himself at home in our meeting. A spiritual son named Paul Yadao (you'll hear his story later in this book) and I were ministering to about four hundred Norwegian men, and the Father's presence was there. He was healing hearts and minds and bodies as we released His love and power.

He was showing up in wonderful ways.

It had been a long day, and I was tired. But the Holy Spirit let me know we were not quite done yet. Eight stoic Norwegian men came up to me. "What would you like Jesus to do for you?" I asked.

They wanted me to release a baptism of love over them. This was not an unusual request. I have spoken and written a lot about the baptism of love God gave me many years ago, I have focused often on encounters with His love in my ministry, and I have been called an ambassador of love in places where love is very hard to see. So I have prayed many times for people to have similar encounters and experiences with His love.

But this time was different.

Something stopped me from praying for these men immediately. I felt a prompt from the Holy Spirit, and a question came to mind: *Would you like a seed or a waterfall? Do you want me to pray and release waves of love over you? Do you want that kind of encounter? Or do you want me to plant a seed of love into the soil of your spirit so it can grow?*

I had never used those words with this experience before.

A waterfall or a seed? A birthing encounter or a process of growth? Was there something missing in the way I had been praying?

Encounters with the Father's love are a very important part of our journey with Him. I was baptized in God's love at a small gathering in Florida in 2000. A worship leader sang a song of the Father's love over me, and I hit the floor. I lay there weeping, feeling the liquid love of the Father flowing back and forth in my body. God performed spiritual surgery on me in that moment. He healed wounds and scars that I had had since childhood. I sensed that I was being totally, completely immersed in the perfect, pure love of the Father. It changed me forever.

That was a beautiful encounter, but I knew that my baptism of love was not just an encounter. I had already been going through a process with God—for years. And I have continued to go through a process with Him ever since. This dramatic revelation of love was a birthing moment in a lifelong adventure, not just a one-time experience.

I think it's wonderful to have encounters with God's love. We all love and long for experiences like that. They have obviously been very significant in my journey with God. I can't imagine what my life and ministry would be like without them.

When I pray and release the Father's love over people, about 10 percent of them have some kind of major encounter like this. They can tell immediately from this birthing experience that something has changed.

But about 90 percent receive the Father's love in seed form. And since that night in Norway, I've realized that the ones who got the "birthing" in that moment had already been in some kind of process with the Father.

Those who got the seed were about to begin a process with Him, which ought to have been very exciting. But if they didn't know what was happening, they might have looked around, seen other people getting the big breakthrough, and been very disappointed.

And those who did get their breakthrough moment might not have known what to do with it once they got home.

All of it is important, and all of it is good—the breakthrough encounters, the growth processes, everything. But most people are just looking for the big moment.

Encounters can be life changing, but just living from encounter to encounter does not bring lasting change. It equips us to live on mountaintops but does not empower us in the valleys. We actually need the whole journey. We need the seeds of experience to multiply in our own lives and bear fruit in our marriages, family relationships, workplaces, and everywhere else we go.

That's how seeds work. They germinate and begin to grow roots. They weather storms and grow strong and tall. Eventually they become trees and produce their own seeds, and you end up not just with a seed or a tree but with a whole forest.

Imagine what that looks like—a seed of love that grows into a tree of love. Others get to taste the fruit of that love, and like all things that are fruitful and multiply, you reproduce yourself. You multiply what you become in your family, your church, your workplace, and your community. You create a force of love that grows and grows and expands infinitely beyond an encounter for one person.

In that meeting in Norway the whole picture of a seed and its growth into a tree that bears fruit and a forest that multiplies came to me in a moment, which is usually a good sign that the Holy Spirit is downloading a new insight. I was surprised by my own words when I asked those men if they wanted the one-time experience or the lasting seed. They were surprised too.

People often come to ministry events hoping for an encounter without seeing the bigger picture. They are looking for the birthing experience—a brand-new event that changes things for them forever. But they sometimes forget what goes into a birth:

- the pregnancy of expectation
- the labor pains that lead up to it
- the nurturing that has to happen for years afterward
- the stewarding of responsibility and the strength to carry it out

Births are wonderful. But they aren't the whole story.

Encounters with God are powerful. They've changed my life. But the context of encounter is process, and we need to have both.

So I prayed that these eight Norwegian men would have more than an encounter. I wanted them to have the encounter, of course, and they did. But more than that, I wanted to plant a seed of love that would take root, be grounded within them, bear fruit in their own lives, and reach into the lives of many others.

I began to envision an entire movement of love.

I believe this is God's purpose for the world—a vast movement of love. He wants to reveal His love to every person, and He wants to do it through people who have experienced it. He wants a love reformation that produces an army of love ambassadors to demonstrate the Father's heart to His world.

Sounds wonderful, doesn't it? This is the kind movement the world needs.

But it cannot happen until we are immersed in the Father's love. We will not see the transformation we hope for in this world until that transformation happens in our own hearts. God's purpose for each of His children and for everyone in this world is to receive love, become love, and release love.

God actually modeled this process for us and then empowered us to live it out—with life-changing, world-changing effects. We will explore that throughout the pages of this book. He is the ultimate ambassador of love who has given us everything we need to become ambassadors of love ourselves.

This "becoming" begins with "receiving." It will involve encounters, and it will also involve a journey. Like every other child of God, you will need powerful, transforming face-to-face experiences with the Father so you can receive His love. But you also need transformation that lasts, that empowers you to live as His beloved son or daughter in whom He is well pleased.

You will need to know in the ups and downs of life that you live, breathe, move, work, and relate in an environment of perfect love.

Did you know that? Yes, as a believer in Jesus, you are already fully accepted. The Father delights in you. You wake up every morning to His smile. He has given you the family robe and the ring of His authority. You have an A-plus on your report card before you even take the test. You are completely, thoroughly, totally immersed in the pure, perfect, eternal love of God.

Fully accepting, receiving, and applying that love is a lifelong journey. This book is a guide, a road map for that journey.

In the following chapters, we will look up and see the perfect love of the perfect family. Then we will look in and see how love entered this world in human flesh and will do the same through each of us. And we will see how love continues to be incarnated in the sons and daughters of God who are being raised up as His love ambassadors.

This upward, inward, outward gaze reveals the foundation, the incarnation, and the calling of love. This is God's purpose for you. And it will change your life and your world forever.

UP

Do you want to understand love?

I think everyone does. It's a big subject, and a mystifying one too. People have been trying to figure love out for thousands of years. We experience it, talk about it, promise it, marry because of it, share it with our friends, pour it out in ministry, and feel it very deeply. We can often see what love looks like. But we have difficulty defining it. It is much bigger than we are, and words are just not enough to capture what it really is.

But God has given us a revelation of it. The loving heart of the Father has been shown to us in Scripture and in the flesh. So if we want to understand love, we should start at the source. We need to go back to the beginning.

That will make much more sense than trying to figure out what love is by looking at it through modern culture, the lyrics of our love songs, or even our own language. After all, we say we love a juicy steak, a spring day, a football team, a hairstyle, a summer breeze, anything in our favorite color, and whatever else makes us happy. But we also love our spouses, our children, and our Lord. Once when I told my wife that I love her, she pointed out that I had just said the same thing about several nice cars. She just wanted to make sure I meant something different by it.

Obviously, not all our loves are the same kinds of loves. They make us have different feelings and come in many shades and intensities. Love has many layers of meaning. But in English, we use the same word for all of them.

Biblical writers didn't. In Greek, for example, there were several words for *love*: *agape, phileo, eros,* and *storge.* Family or natural, instinctive love (*storge*) is different from the bonds of brotherly love (*phileo*), which is different from romantic love (*eros*). And none of them was understood to be as deep and lasting as the unconditional love that is rooted more in the one who loves than in the one who is loved (*agape*).

If we were to put all of these different kinds of loves together, with agape leading the way, we would start to get a sense of God's love; He invented them and invited us to experience them all. But we still cannot quite capture His kind of love in language. The closest we can come to understanding it is through pictures.

So, let's start with some pictures. We will go back to the beginning, to the source, into the beauty, depth, power, and glory of the measureless, priceless, eternal love that existed before the world began.

We are not seeking to love and be loved naturally to the best of our ability. That can be good, but it will never be enough.

We want to love and be loved supernaturally. So digging down into the human heart will not help us find what we're looking for. We need to look up, into the heart of God, the Creator of this universe who *is* love.

Let's begin this journey there, with our eyes gazing above.

CHAPTER 1

THE FAMILY OF LOVE

Have you ever thought about where love comes from?

If you have, you probably assume it comes from God. And you'd be right. It does.

But God has never been a lonely being who existed by Himself before He created anything. For one thing, He is eternal, which means He is outside of time. Technically, there is no "before" with God.

But there's another reason God has never been by Himself.

In the beginning, there was (and still is) a family: the Father, the Son, and the Holy Spirit. And this family is not only the perfect expression of love. This family *is* love.[1]

So when we think about where love originally came from, it isn't from the heart of a God that lives by Himself. It's from the heart of a divine relationship, even from the start. It's a family kind of love that is more perfect than we can possibly imagine.

When we understand this perfect family love, the whole idea of an angry, critical God that so many people have begins to fall apart. I spent much of my life thinking of God as very stern and authoritative, as though He was always focused on my faults. No matter how hard I tried, I assumed that His priority for me was to improve me in whatever areas I was falling short. I always felt like I needed to get cleaned up and put everything in order before He could really use me and relate to me. In my mind, He always seemed a little frustrated with His people—and specifically with me.

But love doesn't focus on those flaws and shortcomings. God wants the best for us, but the best begins with delight and adoration. Anger doesn't produce the best in people. Kindness and compassion do.

So this family is not angry by nature. The Father, Son, and Spirit are not frustrated. They don't sit around talking about how bad things are or how disappointed they are.

There has never been any jealousy or competition in this family. No striving for rights, no complaints about injustice, no bickering about who gets what.

No member of this family has ever wondered, "Why don't I get to be like Him? Why do You give Him more than You give Me? When do I get My turn?"

Can you imagine what would happen if you asked the Father, the Son, or the Spirit which one of them was most important? How would they answer? I can't imagine any of them stepping up and claiming to be in first place. I think they would all point to one another.

None of these family members has ever felt disconnected or distant from another, simply because They are one. You can't have disconnection and distance in a three-in-one person.

Because of this perfect unity, no member of this family has ever felt insecure or needed more attention or affirmation. No one has tried to pose as someone He isn't in order to make Himself feel better. None has ever had to develop coping skills or needed healing from emotional wounds. None has ever worried that love will run out.

The Father, Son, and Spirit are an eternal family with an eternal love.

But beings with eternal love can't be content to keep it to themselves. The beauty of love is always realized in its expression and demonstration. It doesn't sit still. It looks for someone who can receive all its wonderful blessings.

The perfect love of this divine family is expressed and celebrated. It is always perfect and always flowing freely. It is always unbreakable but always determined to fulfill one another's desires and purposes, which are in complete harmony. It's constant but always moving, never seasonal but always looking for seasons of opportunity and growth, fully satisfied but always hungry for more.

And in all those truths—those paradoxes of perfect love—it longs for expression. Love seeks manifestations, looking for ways to bring others in. If perfect love is selfless, it will find a way to turn toward other selves.

That's the nature of our triune God. His Kingdom exists *because of* love and *for* love because He *is* love. The culture of this Kingdom is thoroughly shaped by the unbreakable union of the divine family, the perfect environment. And everything in His Kingdom, whether visible or invisible, eternal or temporal, overwhelmingly beautiful or ordinary and mundane, exists because of love.

Every good thing finds its source in love.

Every good thing is sustained by love, or more specifically, by the One who is love, the Father who loves perfectly.

And all of His attributes find their fullness and perfection in love.

That tells us a lot about ourselves. If every good thing is sourced by and sustained by love, and we are a *"very good"* thing (Genesis 1:31), then we find our source, our sustenance, and our reason for being in this foundation of love.

We'll talk more about creation soon, but just think for a moment about the fact that human beings exist because of love. The first verse of the Bible says, *"In the beginning God..."* (Genesis 1:1), and if God is love, we are justified in reading that verse as, "In the beginning love...."

Many Christians are still very focused on sin and brokenness, even though these are exactly the problems Jesus came to heal us from. And I know from experience that when you are focused on sin and brokenness, you have a tendency to see God as angry and authoritative, maybe with His arms crossed or His head shaking in disapproval. I did, so I understand what that's like. You see a God who is hard to please.

That is not the picture of God that the Bible gives us. This is not the heart behind creation. This was no part of the heavenly family's love. Before the foundation of the world, there was love.

And if you read Scripture carefully, you'll see that this is when the remedy for sin was already planned. God chose us *"before the foundation of the world"* to be holy and blameless in

Jesus (Ephesians 1:4). Looking ahead over all the rebellion in the world into each of our lives, even before it all happened, God said yes to love.

This is what our Father's heart looks like. This is the picture He gives us.

Before the world was made, it was already in God's mind to bring created beings into the fellowship of the divine family. He was motivated to express His true nature—not only within the Trinity but far beyond it. So love went to work to create a beautiful, harmonious, joyful expression of His goodness.

In other words, this world exists because God wanted to make His love visible.

Love Before Time

Love always has this desire to flow outward. People who are able to develop a warm, welcoming, accepting environment in their home enjoy inviting others into it. Artists who put their creativity and skill into a masterpiece want to share it with other people. Families who celebrate and value each member's joys, successes, personalities, and gifts have a way of bringing others into that celebration and joy.

Love is a beautiful thing, but no one sees how beautiful it is unless it is expressed. It needs to be demonstrated to be appreciated.

The warmth, peace, joy, and love of the heavenly family were too wonderful not to be shared. Papa God opened the doors of His living room so many could come in and experience the delight of His love. The Son welcomed many brothers and sisters. The Holy Spirit fills the whole environment.

So the atmosphere of Heaven is full of life and laughter. There is no shame or fear there, no brokenness, no pain. It is a place of deep affection and intimacy, waiting to be shared.

This is the story behind Father, Son, and Spirit's brilliant idea to make human beings in their image. They wanted to create a place on earth that looks like Heaven, where love and honor flourish in the same way it does in the family of Heaven. So God created a garden named Eden. If you've ever wondered what God's house might look like if it were in your neighborhood, this is it. The blueprint of His home is a beautiful garden with an atmosphere of love.

In this perfect atmosphere, God did something that would change the universe for all time. He picked up some dust, shaped it into a familiar form, and exhaled on it. He made an image of Himself, a form like the face of Jesus, and breathed the Spirit into its nostrils. The whole heavenly Family was involved in creating this first member of the earthly family.

When Adam opened his eyes for the very first time, he was looking straight into the face of his Father. He felt his Papa's breath. He heard his Papa's voice. He saw his Papa's smile and felt His love.

From the start, Adam knew the fellowship of the Trinity in this wonderful perfection of the garden. He sensed the first family's presence. He was created in an atmosphere of perfect love.

The fact that Adam was created in the Garden of Eden means he was placed right in the middle of the pleasure and delight of the Father—a template for every human being, the foundation we need to remember whenever our hearts question the Father's love. The first man was placed in the perfect environment in an atmosphere of love. From the beginning until now, every one of us exists for His pleasure and delight.

So that's our picture. Love was the divine motivation behind this creation. Each member of the Trinity was involved in the genesis of this world—the Father who spoke it into being, the Son by whom and for whom it was made, the Spirit who hovered over the waters and who was the breath of life entering into the first man. Each member was there when human beings were formed.

Everything God did in creation was the fruit of this harmonious, loving relationship in the perfect family of love.

Even that troublesome tree.

This is a fascinating plot twist in the story of creation. Have you ever wondered why a loving Father who delights in His children would put two trees right in the middle of the garden and then forbid His beloved children from eating from one of them? Why wouldn't He just put the tree of life there and plant the tree of the knowledge of good and evil far, far away—or leave it out altogether? Why would a good Papa even invite that temptation?

Many people have wrestled with that question. Whole theologies have been developed to separate God from this very dangerous, seductive part of His creation. And we can understand why. This a very curious and intriguing puzzle.

So what's the answer? Why would Papa God put the catalyst for humanity's terrible fall right in the middle of the perfect environment created by His love?

Because love is not real unless it is chosen.

The Father, Son, and Holy Spirit choose to love one another. This is their nature, but it's also their choice. No one in the environment of Heaven compels the Trinity to "act" loving or even to "be" loving. They just are. They don't ever have to remind one another of a command to *"love one another."* Human beings may need that reminder from time to time, but it's supposed to become our nature, just like it is the nature of the Father, Son, and Holy Spirit.

If love is forced, it is not love.

And just as love is not authentic if it's forced, it also is not authentic if it's the only option.

Have you ever thought about how little our love for God would mean if we did not have any other choice? If the first humans knew no one but God and loved Him simply because they had no alternatives, their love would not resemble the love of Heaven. The omniscient Trinity could envision all kinds of alternatives and still chose love over all of them. Adam and Eve could not demonstrate that same kind of love without knowing about other options.

God did not want human beings to be robots in their affection. It had to be real. And to be real, it had to be chosen.

You will see this principle at work in your life very often. There will always be trees in the garden of your life that offer alternatives to your love for God—or even your love of anyone and anything else. The good news is that you get to choose the affections of your heart.

But there are two sides to that coin. Along with the opportunity to choose your affections, there is also a challenge that comes with it. You are *responsible* for choosing the affections of your heart. Human beings are given options so our love will be freely given.

So even back at the very the beginning, perfect love gave free will to the beloved. No area of creation was left out of His loving touch. Every aspect of this world—even that tree—was an expression of the heart of the Father.

Sounds kind of risky, doesn't it? Didn't God have a lot at stake by placing a forbidden tree right in front of Adam's and Eve's faces?

Yes.

If you have ever loved someone deeply, you have probably noticed that love can make you very vulnerable. Love takes risks. It opens your heart to be wonderfully fulfilled, but it also opens you up to become seriously wounded. You can experience unconditional acceptance, but you can also experience painful rejection. When love is both given and returned, it is one of the most satisfying experiences a person can have, but when you enter into that kind of relationship, you know you might get hurt.

In a very real sense, God made Himself vulnerable to the affections of His own creation.[2] He created human beings—in His image so we could receive and give His kind of love—knowing that many would love Him and many would reject Him. He saw it all ahead of time, including the solution for everything that would go wrong. He saw the enormous sacrifice He would make to bring a rebellious world back into the love of the divine family.

And He chose you. If every aspect of this world was an expression of the heart of the Father, and if He knew all things in advance, He knew you before it all began.

Take some time to let that sink in. You, with all of your personality, gifts, appearance, experiences, mistakes, and opportunities, were known before time began.

Who were you before the foundation of the world? What did Papa God see when He looked ahead and saw you? Did He see you the same way you see yourself today?

No. Not at all. He didn't see you the way you see you. He didn't love you the way you love (or don't love) yourself. He saw you with perfect delight. He saw clearly, purely, lovingly into the true you. He knew then and He knows even now the real you as you were created and designed to be.

As we will see, this is where your identity is found. His vision of you from the beginning—before all the flaws and mistakes and insecurities and fears—is who you really are.

We saw earlier that Paul pointed to all of this—the big story of creation and your individual story—in the New Testament. *"He chose us in Him before the foundation of the world, that we should be holy and without blame before Him in love"* (Ephesians 1:4).

A couple of chapters after this insight, Paul prayed that his readers would be given much internal strength. They would need it to be able to handle the enormity—the width, length, depth, and height—of the love of Christ and to be filled with the fullness of God. (See Ephesians 3:16–19.) This love is like a vast ocean of limitless dimensions. It simply cannot be measured.

In other words, Papa God's love is so great that we cannot receive it unless He gives us the supernatural ability to take it in.

Before He spoke this world into being, God already saw the beauty of creation, the love and rebellion of human beings, the redemption He was planning to accomplish, and all the people who would be restored as sons and daughters in His love. He saw it all, and He still went ahead with it. He had His reasons, and they were all very good.

Immersing us in His love—to the point that we would be filled, overflowing, and overwhelmed with it—has always been His plan.

Notes

1. John makes the famous statement that "God is love" in chapter 4, verse 8 of his first letter. In case his readers missed it, he repeats it again in verse 16.

2. God is not deficient in anything and cannot be harmed, but Scripture is clear that He can feel grief, sorrow, and the pain of rejection.

CHAPTER 2

CREATED IN LOVE

What is the most breathtaking sight you've ever seen?

Maybe you love the mountains—how they reach into the clouds and tower over beautiful river valleys below. Maybe you're a beach person—you can't resist a colorful sunset over a peaceful sea. Perhaps you're captivated by the mystery of life—seeing a newborn baby gaze into its mother's and father's eyes.

Whatever your favorite scenes are, you know how beauty can overwhelm you. You know what it's like to see something amazingly beautiful and let your heart be captured by it.

Whatever that picture is for you, there is love behind it. Creation is the reflection of God's glory and an expression of His love. The beautiful sights, the captivating sounds, the sweet tastes and smells, the tender touches—all of these wonderful things come from the heart of the Father as gifts to His beloved sons and daughters who are made in His image. This master artist has painted gorgeous views and created pleasant experiences all around us.

Eden was the canvas of God's love, and God did more than paint beautiful scenes there. He created a setting for something much deeper and even more meaningful. This is where He could reproduce the kind of relationship that characterized the heavenly family, where sons and daughters could live out their calling as images of His nature. He created human beings to look like Him, to live like Him, and to love like Him. He blessed them and told them to be fruitful, multiply, fill the earth, and take dominion over it. (See Genesis 1:26–28.)

In this landscape of love, the relationships of the first family were meant to reflect divine values, their work was meant to further Papa God's purposes, and their hearts were meant to align with each other's hearts. There would be no insecurity, animosity, competition, emotional wounds, distorted thoughts, dishonest words, or impure motives. This human family had the potential to live in a world where racism, exploitation, poverty, slavery, injustice, and disease were unheard of; they were strange, foreign concepts.

We know this is not how it turned out, of course. But for a moment, just imagine that it did. What would this world look like if it truly reflected the love and glory of God? What would our lives be like without any of the self-centeredness that came in at the fall? What if everyone loved one another as perfectly as the heavenly family loves us—if there was no jealousy and no rivalry, and if everyone always fully supported one another's God-given dreams and desires?

Many great thinkers have tried to envision a world like this—a utopia, a paradise, a fantasy world for dreamers and visionaries to think about, all stirring up some deep desires within our hearts. But these scenes are very different from life as we know it.

Our world could have been like that, but tempted human beings made a bad choice. We mistrusted the perfect family's love. We have all opted for self over selflessness. We have eaten from the wrong trees.

Why?

That is a very complicated story, and it's a little obscure. But the Bible gives us hints about it.

Based on those hints, if we were able to peek into Heaven before time, I think we would see one particular created being who didn't "get" what love was all about. He did not love himself the way the Father loved him. He did not recognize who he was. He was not content simply to be loved and to love in return. He broke the covenant and violated the family culture. He went his own way.

This one act of opting out of the divine family's love has created all kinds of problems in the world. It looked like self-promotion, and that's how it was intended. But in reality it was an act of self-sabotage.

This beautiful, created being decided he wanted "greatness" instead of love. He chose the glory of self instead of the glory of all. He cut off outward love and turned it around so it was directed completely inward.

This angelic rebellion was a violation of the perfect environment of Heaven and an assault on the perfect family. And this is where our story, though we weren't yet living it at the time, took a bad turn.

That is the root of self-promotion, self-protection, and self-will in this world. These things came from one rebellious heart before the world began.

Can you see that? All of the world's problems...

All of the heartache and pain...

All of the turmoil and conflict...

All of the exploitation and abuses...

All of the emotional wounds and scars...

All of the aching and weeping and desperate cries...

Everything that is broken came from a created being who lost sight of perfect love—who did not know how to be loved, and therefore did not know how to love, and therefore left the warmth of the Father's living room and tried to build his own kingdom.

Everything wrong with this world happened because someone opted out of love. And then he tricked the first human beings into opting out of love too.

This is where the rebellion against love entered into creation, but for a moment look back before that time. As we saw in the last chapter, Papa God knew each of us before the world was made.

So who were you then? Even before you knew yourself, what did your Father know to be true of you? What was your original design? What was your personality, your gifts, your special nature supposed to be like in the perfect environment of the perfect family's love? Where were you intended to sit in that warm, affectionate gathering in the Father's living room?

To answer those questions, you might need to ask God for a revelation, because it involves things we cannot know by natural wisdom and understanding. But we can know what we've already been told. We can put the pieces of the story together.

And we know that God saw each of us, including you, with very good intentions and a beautiful plan.

We know that, in His omniscience, He could already see everything you regret and the things you don't like about yourself. And He still saw a true you, a perfect design, a redeemed purpose, a glory and destiny for you to walk in.

We know that, in His love, He already had a plan for forgiving, redeeming, and restoring every one of His people.

I hope you see what this means for you. It means that your story did not just begin when you were born or even when you were conceived. Your journey goes much further back than your memory or the memory of your parents and grandparents.

The real you, the original you, was in the heart of Papa God before time. So if you really want to know where your journey begins, you have to start there.

Yes, the fall of humanity and the sins of the world took that journey in some very unpleasant directions. Your sins have played a big part in that too. You are probably well aware of some of the ways you have taken the wrong turn. In fact, if you're like most people, you have probably let your insecurities and regrets define you, as if your past is all the evidence you need of the real you.

But none of your sins, mistakes, flaws, failures, offenses, fears, and insecurities—no other sources of guilt and shame, no matter how long they have weighed on you—define your story. From God's perspective, they are intrusions on your journey.

They came very late in the process—long after He already defined the true you in His own heart.

So if you really want to know who you are, you have to look back at the love before time. And you need to see yourself in the heart of your Father and know that all of His purposes were beautiful and good.

Go back for a minute to those breathtaking scenes that began this chapter. All of that beauty, all of the divine kindness and creativity that went into the master artist's work, all of the love poured into creation—you are part of that.

When God spoke over creation and said it was *"very good,"* He was thinking about you (Genesis 1:31).

You were designed to fit into the glory of the garden, even if you came long after it.

The heart of Papa God looked ahead and saw His initial creation as good and beautiful. He loved all of it, even from the start.

That does not mean He loves all the sin and rebellion that has taken place. But when we're talking about the true you, the person who was in the heart of the Father as He looked ahead to your day, we're not including sin and rebellion. Those are distortions. Your identity is outside of them because God's thoughts of you came before they did.

In God's mind, His idea of who you are fit within His idea of the perfect environment of the garden and everything else He created in love.

This is why we need restoration. The Gospel includes forgiveness of our sins and healing from sin's consequences, but it is bigger than that. It's about restoring us back into the image God envisioned for us before time began.

This means that not only does our journey begin in the heart of the Father before the foundation of the world, it ends there too. Our destination is in the same heart, both from before time and when time is over. From start to finish, the love of God sees who we are and is constantly leading us into our true selves.

His love is always there, never changing, never wavering, measureless and timeless, always sustaining, always pursuing.

When the first human beings opted out of love—just like the orphan spirit who deceived them had done—God did not stop loving them. He had made them in His image so they could fellowship with Him. His love did not stop flowing.

He did drive them from the garden, which might seem like an angry thing to do. But even that was an act of love. Can you imagine what the human race would be like if they had eaten from the tree of life while still infected with the fruit of sin? That would be an even worse disaster than the fall. We would have everlasting life in a rebellious state or an eternity without love.

No, that just couldn't be allowed to happen. So God separated them from that tree of life for a time.

Another kind of tree of life would be needed, one that could take away sin while also offering eternal life. One that could make life last forever again but put an expiration date on evil.

One that could restore us to our true selves as Papa God created us to be.

One that could bring us back into a beautiful, lasting experience of His love.

CHAPTER 3

THE SEEDS OF THE FALL

I gave my life to Jesus when I was thirteen, but I still carried a lot of pain in the years that followed. And pain always seeks pleasure.[1] So when some friends introduced me to some very unhealthy habits, I gave in to them. My search for love took me further away from it.

That is often what the emptiness in our hearts does to us. It drives us to reach out for love. But because the eyes of our hearts have a hard time recognizing the real thing, we take whatever looks like it, even if it carries us further away.

I ended up spending much of my time in a park in Oslo, Norway, broken and filled with guilt and shame. I knew I had forsaken God and my family. I knew I didn't deserve anything from them, but I also knew I had to go home. I needed relief.

My family was amazing. They welcomed me with open arms, even though I had hurt them deeply. It was a wonderful experience, a lot like being invited into the warmth of the divine family's love.

Still, I knew something was missing. I turned back toward Jesus, but now I began serving Him to be accepted by Him. I worked very hard at becoming a son of the Father. I went into ministry and served in churches, pouring out my life as faithfully as I could. I did not realize I was still looking for love. I needed to be filled up, but instead of filling myself up with those bad habits and empty pleasures of before, I was trying to fill myself up with things I knew God would like. I was trying to do something to get something to be someone.

That's how our craving for love works. That is the lie Adam and Eve bought into in the garden. They were told they needed to do something to get something so they could be someone. They forgot that they already were someone, had already been given everything, and did not have to do anything to please their Father.

Once we have stepped out of the environment of Papa God's love, our craving to get back into it drives us toward one of two things: (1) distorted desires and pleasures that blind us to God or (2) performance and works in an effort to please Him.

One way or another, we're trying to get attention, soothe our pain, and fill up on whatever is missing in our hearts. We strive for the love we were created for because we forget how loved we already are.

The reality is that we do not actually need to do anything to get something and be somebody. God has already done everything and given everything because we already are somebodies in His eyes. The seeds of the enemy that were sown into human hearts long ago in Eden have blinded us to that truth.

The Broken Image

"Has God really said?" (Genesis 3:1 NASB). That is how the enemy sowed these seeds into the heart of mankind. When our first parents listened to that question, it became the seed that grew into dense forests of deception in our lives.

This is where our separation from God began—not separation from His love, but separation from being able to receive it and experience it the way He wanted us to.

Guilt, shame, broken identity, broken relationships, and all the other disappointments and diseases of a fallen life entered in. We lost the ability in our natural selves to receive and give divine love and express it to one another.

Adam and Eve listened to the wrong voice, and self rather than Papa God became the center of every human being's life.

We still have many problems with that. We have inner voices of condemnation and shame that are not holy. They might sound humble, but they contradict what God has said about us in Jesus.

They are the voices of the accuser turning us inward, keeping us focused on ourselves. And those voices can be loud and relentless.

What happens when self is at the center of our lives? Love becomes transactional rather than relational. We do things in order to get it. We have to perform well for it—to behave ourselves, live up to a high standard, or whatever our instincts tell us we have to do in order to deserve it. And since we can never do enough to deserve the perfect love of the heavenly family—it is never about "deserving" anyway—we are always striving and never arriving.

I call this a "love vacuum"—an empty heart that is desperate to be filled with the Father's love. Every human being since the fall starts out with one. We live from a love deficit.

In itself, this is a tragic situation. But it has even more tragic consequences because whenever love is absent, fear flourishes.

I think you are probably familiar with the fruits of fear. When we are afraid, we compensate by trying to fend for ourselves, control our lives, become self-protective, and create boundaries and distance between us and other people.

Deep inside of every independent, isolated, overassertive, manipulative person is a heart that is deeply ashamed, starving for affirmation, and very afraid.

Over time, these seeds of our Father hunger grow. They cause insecurity, low self-esteem, self-hatred, violence, paranoia, anger, suicidal thoughts, promiscuity, rebellion, confusion, restlessness, depression, addictions, compulsive behavior, mental problems, and so much more. People spend years in counseling for these kinds of things, never realizing the root behind them.

We need the love of the Father.

If we are unaware of His love—or even if we are aware but not fully convinced of it—we live like orphans.

The Orphan Heart

I once spoke to a group of psychiatrists. Some of them were professors at top universities. I explained this root of our insecurities. I told them that everyone, no matter what their exterior looks like, knows the feeling of failure. No matter how hard they try, no one ever feels like they measure up.

Several of these psychiatrists began to weep. Many of them recognized these symptoms in their hardest, most hopeless cases. Some of them recognized them in themselves. Our Father hunger is universal. We were all created to know the love of the perfect family.

Our human instincts and ingrained assumptions go to war against our desire to fully accept the Father's love. That is not the way we were designed; these instincts and assumptions were not given by God and came only after the fall. But basically we have been conditioned to assume that when we've fallen short—sinned, failed, not measured up—God withholds a little bit of love from us, and only when we are doing everything well in our relationships, personal habits, and attitudes can we be fully at rest in His love.

The problem with that idea should be obvious. It means we are never quite measuring up. So we can never be at rest.

But if Papa God's love is that highest form of agape, then it is not dependent on our behavior or attitudes at all. He might care about those things, but He will never measure His love by them.

His love is completely independent, based entirely on His character and nature, and therefore unchanging, constant, full, deep, and permanent.

But we still have a lot of trouble accepting that.

Maybe you are thinking that your inability to measure up means that Papa God is not completely delighted in you all the time—that even though He loves you, maybe you're a problem child, and He only loves you because He has to. It's His job description, kind of like a parent or grandparent has to accept you as part of the family even if they are upset with you. When we see God through the assumption that His love is an obligation, we can never really understand the pleasure He gets from loving us.

We need supernatural help to comprehend this. We need revelations and encounters and mountaintop moments when the Holy Spirit deposits this new paradigm deep into our hearts. It really is radical, even though it has been there from the very beginning. And it takes some radical heart surgery for us to accept it.

If you have ever read the Book of Ecclesiastes, you may have noticed a lot of this Father hunger between the lines on the page. Apparently written by Solomon (though his name isn't mentioned in it), this book describes the futility of a world that doesn't know the love of the Father.

> *Utterly meaningless! Everything is meaningless* (Ecclesiastes 1:2 NIV).
>
> *What do people gain from all their labors?* (Ecclesiastes 1:3 NIV)
>
> *All things are wearisome* (Ecclesiastes 1:8 NIV).
>
> *The eye never has enough of seeing, nor the ear its fill of hearing* (Ecclesiastes 1:8 NIV).
>
> *What a heavy burden God has laid on mankind!* (Ecclesiastes 1:13 NIV).
>
> *All of them are meaningless, a chasing after the wind* (Ecclesiastes 1:14 NIV).

And these words are just in the first chapter. Nowhere in this book does the writer say anything specific about having a huge wound in his heart or a vacuum that needs to be filled by the Father's love. But he doesn't have to for us to see it.

He has lived long enough, experienced enough things, and tried out enough coping mechanisms to know that life without the Father's love—life *"under the sun"* in this natural, fallen world—is empty (Ecclesiastes 1:9 NIV).

Without that love, the human heart aches. Or dies.

Or it causes us to live like orphans, as though we have to survive on the streets because if we don't take care of ourselves, no one will.

Can you imagine what a world full of insecure orphans would look like? With everyone desperately trying to fill their hearts either with pleasures that substitute for love or with performance anxiety because they never feel like they have earned it?

Actually, you don't have to imagine that, do you? You see it all around you, every day in the news headlines, in your relationships, maybe even in your own heart. There is chaos, corruption, and competition everywhere we look. People have followed the first humans in opting out of the perfect family. Hearts are disconnected from Papa God's love. And when hearts are disconnected, they look for other connections in all kinds of unhealthy ways.

A fascinating story in Genesis 11 captures the results of this orphan spirit. Way back at the very beginning, God had said, *"Let us make man in Our image,"* and then told Adam and Eve to go and fill the earth (Genesis 1:26,28).

But in chapter 11, human beings essentially tried to craft a world in their own image. *"Come, let us build ourselves a city, and a tower whose top is in the heavens,"* they said. *"Let us make a name for ourselves, lest we be scattered abroad over the face of the whole earth"* (Genesis 11:4).

This was a God-given desire turned inside out, the orphan spirit's distortion that makes people think they have to look out for their own interests above all others. The Tower of Babel was an effort to build a name for themselves and to live together and not be scattered—the opposite of what God had told Adam and Eve.

It was a search for things that had already been given. The people at Babel were looking for meaning and trying to find it in a tower that reached into Heaven.

Is there any better picture of the heart silently crying out for the Father's love and not knowing how to receive it?

Before we encounter the love of the heavenly family, we are constantly building our own towers. We reach for something we think will fulfill us. And we think we have to. We do not yet realize that God has reached down to us.

This effort to make a name for themselves is also a search for a missing identity. They did not know they had been created to be sons and daughters of the Father. They didn't remember that they had been made in His image. They were reaching for a name, an identity, a place in the family.

So they tried to create a "name" or an image for themselves.

Just like we do. When we don't know who we are, we posture ourselves to create an image. We strive for fame, recognition, status, individuality—anything that will make us stand out as "somebody."

But when God made mankind in His image, we were automatically somebodies, weren't we? We cannot become any more significant than being a son or daughter of the Most High. Our search for meaning, significance, and our missing identity was already answered before it ever started, but we started it anyway because we just didn't know.

If only the people at Babel had known.

They didn't need a tower for meaning.

They didn't need new image for significance.

They didn't need a name for an identity.

People who know the love of the Father—who are saturated in it, all the way into the depths of their hearts—do not feel the need to build a kingdom for themselves. They don't have to make a name for themselves or create just the right image. They have dreams, desires, and goals, but they are not driven by a desperate need to be somebody because they know they already *are* somebody.

But insecure hearts strive for their own kingdoms. They do not know that by faith they are already members of the royal family.

Insecure hearts think they need to make a name for themselves. They don't know that by faith the Father freely gives His own name to His people. They don't know they can wear the name of the Son and pray in His. Nameless, they go searching for a name that means something to them.

No wonder so many people view the world as a competition—the survival of the fittest. That is how isolated, lonely, disconnected orphan hearts get by.

This build-a-city, make-a-name approach to life finds many expressions in our world. It might take shape as a business, a government, an organization, even a religion. People build and build and build to "make it" in life and to leave a legacy.

Don't misunderstand. There is nothing wrong with building something and leaving a legacy. The issue is whether someone is doing it as a kingdom enterprise or doing it from a desperate need to become somebody. Those who know the Father's love recognize the difference.

These man-made towers, these organizations and systems human beings have created out of an orphan spirit are only sustainable when they are kept under control, and eventually they can no longer be kept completely under control.

Remember, one of the responses of fear is a compulsion to control things. People who are overwhelmed by their circumstances try to control them. People who carry fear into their relationships do whatever they can to control them. Fear is the parent of a controlling spirit.

So man-made towers have to be controlled because they are fundamentally driven by fear and insecurity. They need rules and decrees and constraints. Anything that is not filled with and covered by the love of the Father—anything not created and sustained in that environment of harmony and warmth and acceptance—needs the force of law.

And law without God enslaves.

This is one reason so many people feel caught, trapped, stuck, and stagnant. They are living and working within the world system that has to be governed by man-made law—fear under control. It's a prison with no way out other than the Gospel that sets people free.

We see that everywhere. If you think about it, *anything* without God is a prison.

Man-made kingdoms are enslaving apart from the King of kings.

Prosperity without the presence of God is ultimately poverty.

Success without the Spirit of God ends in failure.

Abundance apart from the ability of God is actually lack.

Spirituality centered on self has nowhere to go for help.

The bottom line is that a world in which everybody is out for themselves is a world with billions of little gods that do not know how to receive divine love or how to give it.

Only God can work the power and glory of perfect love back into such a broken world.

Note

1. Or as a friend puts it: "Our losses crave being filled up with the God of all comfort. Avoiding the pain of feeling our losses sets us on an insatiable road of attempting to fill up our deficits with a counterfeit.…We can use good, beautiful gifts that are intended to make life rich to keep our hearts poor in our losses. If we do not validate our losses and choose to grieve, we create ways to cope with what or who is missing. We are not wired to cope. We are wired for Love that fills us with comfort." (Jennifer Stockman, *Love That Baptizes Our Grief*, unpublished, June 29, 2020.)

CHAPTER 4

HOW GOD WOVE A THREAD OF LOVE THROUGH A TORN WORLD

I woke up one morning in Pakistan to a long and loud call to prayer, and even though I was very tired, I could not go back to sleep. So I turned on the TV and on channel after channel I saw Muslim clerics teaching from their scriptures. *Maybe that will put me back to sleep,* I thought.

I recognized one of the imams I saw from previous trips, and I got a very strong impression that God wanted me to meet this man. That seemed impossible. This man was very famous and well insulated from people like me, an "infidel."

But this was one of those impressions that would not leave. I tried to put it out of my mind, but it kept coming back. I could not get rid of it.

That's often a sign that God is breaking into our thought patterns, trying to get through. *Maybe*, I thought, *I should just give it a try.*

So I tried several ways to contact this teacher, and nothing worked. I had done my best. Now, perhaps, I could just consider this to have been a false impression. Maybe I could put it aside.

But the Holy Spirit spoke again. (He does not just "let it go" like we do.) He reminded me that He had not asked me to *try* to meet this man. He said He wanted me to meet him.

When I finally got to the point of telling the Holy Spirit I had no idea how to do that, I sensed Him saying, "Great, now we can get started." And then I heard the Spirit ask me a question: "When you look at this man, what do you see?"

I had been looking at this Muslim teacher through natural eyes as someone on the other side—as a believer of a false religion or a spiritual adversary.

Papa God had another view of him, and He wanted me to see the way He sees and think the way He thinks. God saw this man before the foundation of the world and rejoiced in His creation. He saw the "true him." He recognized this teacher as a man of peace.

That may be hard for some people to accept, but God sees everyone according to their destiny, not their past. He sees them through eyes of love, not rejection. He saw a young shepherd boy as a future King David. He saw Saul the violent enemy as the apostle Paul. He saw you and me as *"holy and beloved"* long before we ever acted like we were holy and beloved (Colossians 3:12).

And He saw this Muslim as a future man of peace.

When you recognize God's heart in something, you have a choice. You can talk yourself out of responding, or you can align with it.

Letting my heart get in sync with God's heart led to an amazing encounter with this man and a relationship that continues today. I have met hundreds of imams and other Muslim leaders through his connections, and I have learned to see them all as the Father sees them—according to their future identity. I have ended up in meetings where a hundred dark eyes were staring at me suspiciously, and I have seen how love changes the atmosphere. When people sense the love of the Father, their hearts begin to turn toward Him.

That picture of the Father's love surprises many people. As a theology, the love of God always plays well. In practical situations, it goes against what many people expect. To put it another way, there is a very big difference between what we say we believe about God's love and how it often applies in real life.

Many Christians seem to assume that the fall in Eden separated us from God's love. That may not be the way they say it, but they feel as if God's heart turned away from us then. But God's heart has always been turned toward us in unconditional, unchanging, deep, and constant love.

We see that clearly throughout Scripture.

The Father demonstrated His love almost immediately by covering Adam's and Eve's shame. Then He sent them out of Eden so they could not eat of the tree of life and preserve their fallen nature forever.

Adam and Eve's second son seemed to understand love. Abel brought an offering to God from the heart, one that wasn't forced, the first of his flock, the very best he could give. His brother Cain brought one out of duty—*"in the process of time,"* which sounds like it was not much of a priority for him—and God did not accept it (Genesis 4:3).

We might describe those offerings today as "relationship" vs. "religion"—one from a man who saw the heart of God as love and the other who saw God as a judge. One offering that was a "get to," the other that was a "have to." One genuine offering, one obligatory one.

Or, to put it another way, Abel's offering was born of love. Cain's was not.

You have probably seen both of those impulses—the "get to" and the "have to"—at work in your own heart, and you probably already know which one God desires. Abel carried this thread of love forward even after the fall.

So did a man named Enoch, who *"walked with God"* for three hundred years before God *"took him"* (Genesis 5:21–24).

So did Noah, who also *"walked with God"* (Genesis 6:9) and whose family was chosen out of all the others on earth to continue the human race.

So did Abraham, who found favor with God and was chosen to walk with Him and enter into a covenant with Him. This covenant was based on faith, but have you ever tried to have faith in someone you don't love? It does not really work that way. You cannot trust whom you do not love.

It is very hard to divorce faith from love, so we know something about Abraham's love for God simply by the fact that he lived out this journey the way he did. We also know God called Abraham His friend. (See Isaiah 41:8; James 2:23.)

We could go on and on—through Isaac, Jacob, and Joseph, who walked faithfully with God through some of life's hardest ordeals; through Moses, who endured all kinds of hardship in delivering God's people from Egypt but asked to see God's glory and pleaded for God to go with him (see Exodus 33:12–23); and through Rahab, who literally hung scarlet thread (a cord, actually) from her window as a sign of aligning with God and His people.

We see it through David, who was known as a man after God's own heart, and the kings in his line who sought revival in a kingdom that had strayed from God's ways, and through the prophets who declared God's message of love, portraying Him as a lover who had been betrayed by the unfaithfulness of His beloved.

You know where we are heading with this, don't you? The thread of love is woven in every direction through Jesus on the cross, the centerpiece of history, the key to Papa God's restoration of this world back into the heavenly Family and the warmth of His living room forever. But more on that later.

The point is that the Father's love has always driven this story. It is always the backdrop of our human journey.

Even in their worst moments, God's chosen people in the Old Testament were on the receiving end of this unfathomable love. In the midst of Israel's unfaithfulness, rebellion, and apostasy—they pursued the gods of other nations, committing spiritual "adultery" in their relationship with God—the Father still told them that He loved them with an everlasting love and would draw them with His lovingkindness. (See Jeremiah 31:3.)

And even in our worst moments today—those times when we are most likely to run from God and assume that we have been disqualified from His love—He still relentlessly loves us. He opens His arms and says, "Welcome home."

Human beings do not love like that, not by nature, anyway. God's love has no beginning or end—something finite, mortal people cannot really understand. This love is beyond our standards and our comprehension. The only way we can love like that is to receive supernatural love from the Father so thoroughly that we become that kind of love.

One of those prophets who declared God's message of love gives us a great illustration of how foreign to us this kind of love is. Hosea was told by God to marry a woman who would be unfaithful to him. In fact, she would not just be unfaithful in the way we normally think of unfaithfulness. She was a harlot, a prostitute, a woman who sold herself to unworthy lovers.

God's point in this very graphic, heart-wrenching illustration was to demonstrate the kind of unfaithfulness Israel had committed against Him. Hosea had to live out the pain of this unfaithfulness.

I don't know if I could do that. If I were in Hosea's place, I would think this was the end of the relationship. You probably would too. Persistent, intentional adultery violates the covenant of marriage. It's a deal breaker.

But this is not how God's love works. In spite of all their unfaithfulness, *God still chose to take His people back!*[h]

His love really is relentless. The cord of love woven throughout Scripture and history does not have a beginning or an end. That perfect love has always existed.

The Book of Jonah is another Old Testament story that illustrates this persistent love of the Father.

God loved His prophet Jonah. But He also loved the wicked city of Nineveh. This Assyrian capital was the enemy of Israel and known for its violent atrocities. God's call for Jonah to go to Nineveh and preach repentance would be similar to telling someone today to go into the heart of ISIS territory and tell those radicals how much the Father loves them.

That seems to be how Jonah saw it too, and it terrified him. It also made him mad. Why would God care about this enemy city that had been oppressing His chosen people? Jonah could not imagine that, so he went in the opposite direction.

God loved Jonah all the way into the middle of the sea. He loved the sailors who cried out to their gods when a storm threatened to overturn their ship. He loved Jonah all the way back into his calling, even though the prophet still didn't love Nineveh the way God loved Nineveh.

Nineveh repented, God turned away His judgment, and Nineveh experienced an outpouring of grace.

Jonah did not like this turn of events at all. He still had not aligned with the heart of the Father. He pouted over God's incredible mercy. He didn't want grace to be shown to these enemies, even though God had given him grace again and again.

So God tried to teach Jonah a lesson about His compassion, and the book ends with a very open-ended question: Shouldn't mercy be shown to this lost, rebellious city? (See Jonah 4:11.) Shouldn't these people be brought back into their God-given destiny?

This open-ended question, of course, is put to the reader too, as if to say, "Aren't you aware that the Father's love applies even to people like these? So how are you going to respond to that?"

It is a lot like another open-ended question in one of Jesus's parables: Who is your neighbor?[2] If God has two really big commands—to love Him with all our heart and love our neighbor as ourselves (see Matthew 22:36–40)—it might be important for us to give a lot of thought to who our neighbor actually is.

It's natural for us to love and affirm family, friends, and others who seem to be "on our side." But Jesus tells us to go beyond that.

We think we are doing a good job to tolerate the people who offend us or who even just rub us the wrong way.

Don't you feel good when you resist the urge to snap back at someone? When you are offended and you choose to forgive? Those are good responses. But they are just the tip of the iceberg of supernatural love.

The supernatural love of the Father pursues people relentlessly, and He wants to put the same heart within us.

What does that look like?

It is very different from what we're used to.

In one of my other books, I told a story about a terrorist named Ahmad. His mission was to carry liquid explosives into a crowd of "infidels" and set them off.

Ahmad accomplished all of his goals except one. He did not die.

Not only did Ahmad fail to sacrifice his life in this mission. He also woke up in an American military hospital, surrounded by strangers who, he had been conditioned to believe, would humiliate him, torture him, and keep him captive for the rest of his life.

But instead of the stereotype of Americans he expected to see, doctors and nurses cared for him, fed him, eased his pain, and spoke comforting words. While many people would have considered this young man a hardened, irreconcilable enemy, this medical staff treated him with dignity. In spite of his physical pain during his recovery, he recalls it as being a better experience than the pain of his childhood.

He was so affected by this experience that he spends much of his time now teaching young Muslims to turn them away from terrorism. Love transformed him.

Once after speaking at a conference about how God was moving in the Muslim world, a family approached me afterward. The wife was leading her husband by the arm. The man's face was scarred, he was missing an eye, and the eye that remained stared blindly to the side. While serving in the Middle East, an improvised device exploded among his unit and nearly killed him.

This man handed me a check for a thousand dollars because he wanted me to take the kind of love I was talking about to the people who had done this violence to him.

That is transforming love. It's supernatural. It does not hold onto offenses but seeks the best even for enemies.

Where can you get that kind of love? Only by looking back to the beginning—to the love before time. This is the heart of the Father manifesting within someone who understands, first of all, how the thread of love has been woven into his or her life, and then wants to weave it into the lives of others.

You will see a consistent theme throughout this book: we receive the heavenly love from the perfect family, we love Papa God back in return, and then we can give this love to others. We receive love, return love, become love, and release love.

The order of that sequence is important. We cannot return any love we have not received. We cannot give what we do not have. No matter how good we believe God to be, theologically we cannot even love Him if we don't know we have been loved by Him first.[3]

As we will see, once we have been supernaturally loved by Papa God, we can become incarnations of His love as we follow Jesus, who is the supreme incarnation of His love. And then we can manifest supernatural love to the world around us.

Almost every Christian is able to say, "I am loved by God." That is a very true belief. But you are probably well aware that there is a big difference between a mind belief and a heart belief. It is one thing to know you are loved by God. It's another to know how much you are loved and what that love looks like, and then for the knowledge of that love to sink deep into your spirit.

For example, let's take a look at the many expressions of the Father's love in Romans 8. First, there is this completely counterintuitive statement that there is *"no condemnation"* for anyone who is in Christ. (See Romans 8:1.) No remnant of judgment against our sin, no legal consequences in the spirit realm, no pointed finger from God.

Then there is a declaration of our adoption as sons and daughters into the perfect heavenly family. (See Romans 8:14–17.) We are embraced by the family's love. We get to sit in the warmth of the Father's living room. Amazingly, we even get to inherit all the Son's blessings!

Then we are being prayed for by the Spirit and the Son. (See Romans 8:26–27,34.) Can you imagine? The whole heavenly family is having a conversation about you right now, and it's all about working out what is best for you. The Father is hearing prayers about you from the Spirit and the Son.

And then we are given assurance that the Father is working out everything for our good. (See Romans 8:28.) Papa God freely gives us all things. (See Romans 8:32.) We simply cannot be separated from His extravagant love. (See Romans 8:35,39.) In fact, He makes sure that we become conquerors and overcomers in everything we face because of the perfect love that empowers us. (See Romans 8:37.)

To sum up this magnificent chapter—if that were even possible—it tells us again and again that we are fully accepted, fully loved, fully embraced, forever and ever.

That is a bigger statement than "God loves me." It is a very specific, empowering love. It reaches into the depths of our spirit. Because of this unconditional love, we are invited into an environment of complete, unchanging acceptance.

If this is the kind of love we receive, then this is the kind of love we can give. And both sides of that statement have to be supernaturally empowered. We receive supernaturally, and we give supernaturally.

When we grasp the Father's love, we no longer see our sin the same way anymore—as something that turns Him away from us. We see Him running toward us to envelop us in the love of the divine family and bring us back in.

We see the political opposition as friends and neighbors.

We see the annoying neighbor as someone in need of a touch from our Papa's love.

We see the egotistical coworker as someone with deep emotional scars that need to be healed.

We see the radical Muslim as someone whose misguided zeal could be turned around in the right direction once he encounters love.

We see the rabid skinhead, the militant terrorist, the blatantly immoral, and everyone else with serious problems as wounded children walking around in adult bodies, needing the love of the Father.

And when that kind of love fills us and overflows from us, we get to re-present—to present again and again—the same grace, mercy, and love we've received.

No, the fall did not separate us from the Father's love. It made the Father's love hard to see, and He has spent millennia revealing it to us and pursuing us with it. The scarlet thread is still being woven. He is still searching for hearts to align with His—to represent the divine love of the heavenly family on earth because that love is the most powerfully transforming force there is.

Notes

1. To sense the emotional ups and downs of this story, read the first two chapters of Hosea. Notice the shift that occurs at 2:14, and especially God's promise in 2:19–20. This kind

of love is hard to grasp, yet it's still a faint picture of the enormity of the love of our Father in Heaven and Jesus our Bridegroom.

2.   The story of the Good Samaritan begins and ends with this question—and a calling to be a neighbor even to the unlikely and unexpected among us. You can read the full parable in Luke 10:29–37.

3.   This truth is expressed in First John 4:19, which talks about how the Father's love is perfected within us.

CHAPTER 5

WHEN ORPHAN HEARTS FIND THEIR FAMILY

Jacob had a destiny over his life.

That was apparent even from the very start. He was reaching for it as he came out of his mother's womb—grabbing his twin brother's heel, aiming for the birthright and blessing of his father.

Like everyone else in this world, Jacob had father hunger. But he was more of a mama's boy, and his father favored the (barely) firstborn, a man's man, the hunter Esau. So that ache for the father, that love deficiency that craves a father's affirmation, seems to have become even worse through the family dynamics.

Jacob just wanted to be valued by his father, and he kept seeing his brother get all that fatherly attention.

As we have seen, father hunger leads to insecurity and fear. Jacob was driven by this hole in his soul, constantly seeking to fill it up with anything he could—especially with the firstborn's birthright and the father's blessing.

After all, if the older brother is getting all the father's attention, why not go for the things the older brother has?

Through a good bit of manipulation and trickery, Jacob ended up getting both of the things he wanted. He caught his brother Esau in a moment of weakness and got him to exchange the firstborn birthright for a bowl of stew. When his almost-blind father was ready to give the firstborn's blessing, Jacob dressed up like his brother (with his mother's help) and received the words spoken over him as if he had been Esau.

The way God has designed the world, words are powerful. Especially in this ancient culture, they were as good as a written contract. You could not just take them back. A blessing was a blessing, and Jacob got what was intended for Esau.

So Jacob heard everything he wanted to hear from his father, even if his father didn't mean it for him. Yet something was still missing.

This 'is how it is with orphan hearts. If you are striving to make a name for yourself, build a tower, or pursue any other substitute for the Father's approval in that desperate search to fill your heart with love, you find that all of those strategies are never quite satisfying.

If the Father's love has not truly sunk in, the heart is still lacking what it needs. It can be filled with many different pleasures and accomplishments and still be empty.

So Jacob's heart was still hungry. No matter what he had obtained, he was still Jacob.

As Jacob fled to his family's distant original homeland—it is better not to stick around when you've deceived a brother and father like he had done—he laid his weary head on a rock to get some sleep.

And then Jacob had a very unusual dream. He saw angels ascending to and descending from Heaven. And he heard an affirmation not from his earthly father but from *the* Father—a promise that God would bless him and his descendants and be with him until all His promises were fulfilled.

When Jacob woke up, he realized God had been in that place. He even realized he had heard affirming words from the Father.

But from what we can tell as his story continues, his heart still was not healed or filled. He simply had an encounter, a visitation from God.

Until an orphan heart is healed, that's all it can have—a visitation. What we really need is a habitation, not just a visitation. But orphan hearts need a transformation to be able to maintain the affirmation they have been given.

Jacob got his birthright, his blessing, and his encounter with God. But he still had a love deficiency. And wherever there is a love deficiency, there is a God deficiency.

If we fast-forward to the end of Jacob's story, we see him heading toward a big, climactic confrontation with his brother Esau. When we last saw Esau, he had wanted to kill Jacob for stealing his birthright and his blessing. So Jacob was terrified of seeing his brother again. He did not know what to expect. Had Esau hung onto a grudge all these years? Probably.

Orphan hearts assume these kinds of things. They live in fear.

But before Jacob had a confrontation with Esau, he had to have a confrontation with God.

It was a very strange confrontation. Jacob actually entered into a wrestling match with an angel, which is seen by many people as a picture of Jesus in the Old Testament. In any case, the Bible says he wrestled with God.

By all logic, that ought to be a losing battle. Many of us have wrestled with God at times too, and for some amazingly beautiful reason, He allows that kind of interaction. He does not destroy us. He enters into the conversation. I think He actually enjoys the fellowship.

So Jacob wrestled with God, *and he won!* Well, he did not actually defeat God, but he also did not let go and give up. It says he *"prevailed"* (Genesis 32:28).

How did he do that? He got pinned. The angel touched the socket of his hip and incapacitated him. Jacob could not get away, but he also would not let go. In fact, he insisted that he would not let go until God blessed him.

Jacob had always been able to get what he wanted one way or another. Like any other orphan heart, he did whatever he needed to do to survive.

So he deceived. He manipulated. And when he worked for years to get his bride Rachel, his father-in-law tricked him and gave him Rachel's sister. The trickster reaped what he had sown. But he got Rachel anyway by promising to work seven more years.

After all he had been through in his life, after all the things he had gotten for himself, after all the affirmation and abundance God had given him, something was still missing.

The blessing he had gotten from his own father so many years earlier had not healed his orphan heart. Now Jacob asked for a divine blessing from this mysterious figure.

"What is your name?" asked the angel (Genesis 32:27).

Wow. Orphan hearts are always working to make a name for themselves. This is a profound question. What did Jacob think his name was?

"Jacob," he answered. Literally this means "supplanter" or "deceiver." His parents had given him a name appropriate for someone who comes out of the womb grasping for his twin brother's heel.

Names in the Bible are a very big deal. They tell us a lot about the person's character and what God wants to do through his or her life.

Abraham could not be the father of all nations until God changed his name from Abram (exalted father) to Abraham (father of a multitude). His wife, Sarah, needed a name change too, from Sarai (possibly meaning "contentious") to Sarah (princess).

For people to receive everything God wants to give them, they need to learn to see themselves according to their new identity. For us to experience all the blessings of the Gospel, we need to see ourselves as new creations, adopted and fully loved and fully blessed by God in Christ.

So for Jacob to receive all God wanted to do for him—to fulfill those promises given back at Bethel, where Jacob had laid his head on a rock and dreamed—he had to see himself as someone other than a deceiver. He could no longer just be Jacob.

In that place of surrender, where Jacob was pinned to the ground by an angel of God, he got a new name. The place of surrender is always a place of change. You will find that to be true in your life again and again. And Jacob's identity changed from deceiver to Israel—one who contends with God and prevails.

Now Jacob would be able walk in his destiny without defaulting back to his old nature. His orphan heart had been adopted and given a new identity. He no longer needed to make a name for himself; a new name had already been given. I don't think he would have put it in these terms, but he had had an encounter with Papa God's love.

Something changed in that moment. Scripture doesn't go into detail about why Esau was coming with four hundred men but not with a plan to attack. It doesn't tell us exactly why Jacob arranged all the women and children the way he did. But his fear seems to have been gone.

The Father's perfect love casts out fear. (See First John 4:18.) It takes care of the root of fear.

Jacob's root fear for years had been Esau's anger. What if his brother tracked him down and just showed up one day with vengeance on his mind? All that time Jacob spent in a distant land, working and marrying and fathering children, he still remembered the last image he had seen of his brother—a man who wanted to kill him. For all he knew, Esau was now marching toward him with four hundred men with that mission in mind.

But Jacob couldn't run away from his wrestling match with God, and he chose not to run away from Esau now. And the first thing we see from Jacob as Esau approached is genuine humility. He bowed down seven times.

No longer did he believe he had something to prove. He was Israel. He already had an A-plus on his report card. He could just be who he was—which was all new now. No more running because there was no more fear.

Jacob/Israel now began to see himself as God saw him. He was resting in a new identity. As always happens in a baptism of love, he started to love himself the way God loved him because he had received the Father's love. And he was able to love Esau the way God loved him because his heart was no longer an orphan heart and could be filled with the Father's love.

Because he had received love, he could give love.

Jacob's bowing and offering were ways of saying, "Whatever I have is yours. I'm not holding on to anything."

And Esau just embraced him. His heart seems to have been healed too. He did not need to be appeased with all of Jacob's gifts.

But Jacob insisted and made a really remarkable statement: "I have seen your face as though I had seen the face of God, and you were pleased with me."[1]

When you realize you have been transformed by love, you start seeing people differently. You don't define them by their history but by their destiny.

And because you are seeing them differently, they start to see you differently. Esau may have been coming with four hundred men because he was suspicious of his trickster brother or perhaps even with vengeance still on his mind. But the loving face that saw his own face with the Father's love made all those issues irrelevant.

That is the by-product of a heart transformed by love. Because Jacob knew he was now Israel, he manifested a new nature. And because he manifested a new nature, other people saw him differently. Even if Esau was coming to kill Jacob, he wouldn't have found a Jacob there. He found an Israel.

And a major reconciliation between families took place, all because an orphan heart discovered a new identity.

Do you see why it is so important to see yourself through the eyes of the Father rather than your own? Why it's so harmful to keep calling yourself "just a sinner" when the Father has given you a new identity as a new creation and made you into *"the righteousness of God"* (2 Corinthians 5:15,21 NIV)? Why "I'm only human" no longer makes any sense when you have been given great and precious promises that empower you to participate in the divine nature? (See Second Peter 1:3–4.)

Jacob's journey is a beautiful picture of how God wants to change our nature, give us a new name, and transform our vision and relationships. He gives us genuine humility, and out of that humility we love freely and completely, with no agenda or hook. Because the environment has changed in our hearts, we can change the environment around us.

When you have seen the face of God, you can look into the face of every root fear in your life, all of your traumatic and painful experiences, and no longer have any fear. And because you have had an encounter with God, others will look at you and see the face of God. They will have an encounter with Him too. And reconciliation and transformation will be the results.

The Journey of God's Family

Jacob's story did not begin with Jacob, of course. It began with his grandfather Abraham, who also had his name changed and his destiny determined by an encounter with the Father's love.

It's not a coincidence that Genesis 12 follows Genesis 11 (and I am not just talking about the numbers). The man-made kingdoms represented by the Tower of Babel are followed by God's choice of Abram (later Abraham) and his family. In fact, Abram was taken out of that very environment where the Tower of Babel was built. He was called to leave his father's household and start something new.

In other words, God plucked a family out of this build-a-city, make-a-name world and reoriented them to an entirely different way of life—one covered with the love of the Father and built on relationship with Him. In fact, God sealed this relationship with a covenant.

God would later establish a covenant of law with Israel through Moses, but Abraham's covenant was not that kind of covenant. It was much earlier and based on faith, not law. Abraham and his family would be blessed by the divine family and brought back into the love that existed before time. And that love would keep on blessing this family and its generations.

This is what love does—it sees the future and blesses. It sees people not according to their past but according to their destiny. That's why God can make everlasting promises that include future generations throughout time. Love always looks forward.

That forward look was already in Papa God's eyes in Eden, when He promised that the seed of the woman would overcome the seed of the serpent. (See Genesis 3:15.) Those deceptive words that drew Adam and Eve away from love would eventually be overcome by love.

We know how that story of overcoming turned out. The ultimate fulfillment of that promise is in Jesus. And it is absolutely fascinating that the Gospel of Matthew begins with a genealogy that goes all the way back to the first earthly family under the covenant of faith; the Gospel of Luke takes it even further, giving us a genealogy that goes all the way back to the first family—not just the first creature but the first *son*.[2]

Why is that so important? This is one of those hints from God about what He is doing, a sign that points us back to very foundational truths—in this case, the love of the divine family that prompted creation in the first place. When Jesus came as the Son of God, He was coming to restore us back to that original image of being sons and daughters of our Father.

The genealogy of Jesus reminds us of Adam—that original vision of seeing the Father's face, hearing His voice, and calling on His name as a member of His family. We're brought back into the warmth of the Father's living room.

Like an innocent child wrapped in a robe of righteousness, we can gaze into the Father's face and receive the pure, transparent, overwhelming love He has for us. This is a relentless, powerful love, a transforming force that heals our hearts. It radically changes us and removes all of our fears. It completely undoes our orphan spirit.

Hearts that have been steeped in fear are trained to resist that kind of experience. After they sinned, Adam's and Eve's instinct was to run away and hide, not to run into the arms of the Papa God's perfect love. They felt shame—always an enemy of intimacy. The thing we need most is something we no longer embrace naturally. We need to be transformed by love.

Prepare Your Heart for an Encounter

How can we be transformed by love? It's one thing to know about the Father's love, but it's another to actually encounter His love in a way that fills us and saturates us and sinks way down into our hearts.

If you want an encounter with His love, I can tell you three keys to prepare your heart that have helped me. But as you prepare, remember that there's a process, and your encounter can come at any point (or points) along the way, and what that looks like is up to God. With that in mind, get your heart ready in these three ways:

1. Do not let anything get in the way of your pursuit of His love. If you don't have time to prepare, make time. If you don't have room for an encounter, make room.

2. Do not let the lies of the enemy convince you that you are unworthy. God is not hung up on what you have done in the past. He is not keeping His distance because you aren't righteous enough yet. By faith in Jesus, He has already made you righteous and covered whatever you have done. If the enemy tries to tell you that you're unworthy, tell him, "Yes, and the Father loves showing up in the lives of unworthy people." You are ready for His presence.

3. Simply pursue Him. Show up, and He will meet you there. Ask to know His love, to see it fully, and to be filled with it. Persevere in that request. Make it the cry of your heart for life. He will not refuse that desire. He wants to bring every orphan heart back into love.

Luke's Gospel gives us a very powerful picture of what it looks like to be brought back into love. It's a story about—no surprise here—a family.

The story is about two sons. One rebelled against his father, and one served his father very faithfully.[3] The first son demanded his inheritance and went away and wasted it. He had a terrible time, ending up in poverty and eating food that pigs eat.

When he finally came to his senses, he went home—not because he was truly sorry but because he had nowhere else to go. But his father, who saw him coming from a distance, ran in the most undignified way to embrace his son and welcome him home.

Did the father rebuke this wasteful son? No.

Did he make him work off his debt? No.

Did he emphasize how long it was going to take to rebuild trust? No.

He threw the family robe around this son and gave him the ring of family authority—the garments of love and the symbol of authority that comes with it. That's a pretty big welcome home.

The other son—the one who had been working very hard to be good and please his father—heard all this attention the younger son was getting and got angry about it. You can probably understand why. This guy had been doing everything he could to help out the family while his foolish brother had gone off to squander the family's wealth and ruin the family's reputation.

And now this brother is being rewarded? Wow.

But the father opened his arms to this son too. He needed a different kind of "welcome home." Then this father reminded this son of a very big, perspective-shifting truth: *"Son, you are always with me, and all that I have is yours"* (Luke 15:31).

Let that sink in for a moment.

If you have been a prodigal son, you are welcomed home with the Father's open arms, and everything the Father has is yours. He throws the family robe on you and gives you the family's ring of authority. You can enjoy the atmosphere of the heavenly family without fear or condemnation. No one in this perfect environment is going to hold your past over your head.

But there is another side to this story. If you have been the older brother working hard to please the Father, *you have always been with Him, and all that He has is yours.* The issue is not whether you have access to the family estate. The question is: Do you *know* you have access to the family estate? And do you know how to bring that access into your experience? Like the prodigal, you can just come. You can enjoy the atmosphere of the heavenly family too—anytime you would like.

Neither son really understood love, but it was offered to both of them, simply because the father loved giving it.

Maybe you have experience like the younger son. You have run from God and sought all that the world has to offer, then discovered that it wasn't very satisfying after all and returned to your Father.

Or maybe you have experience like the older son, always serving the Father diligently in hopes of hearing a "well done" and receiving your inheritance one day—looking down on your younger brother's foolishness as you work—and remaining disconnected from the Father through it all.

As I explained in my story earlier, I have experience in both roles. I have been both the son who was lost and the son who was working in the fields. I ran from God and sought pleasure to soothe my fear and pain. I also worked hard to prove I was a son, striving to earn my birthright and expecting to receive my inheritance one day by behaving well, preaching the right things, knowing the Word better than anyone else, and competing and performing rather than serving and enjoying.

But as a prodigal on the run, Papa God did not rebuke me for anything I had done wrong when I finally came home. He ran to me and embraced me, just as my earthly father did, and He told me I was His beloved son in whom He was well pleased. I received both His robe and His ring—the family identity and the family authority.

I felt like life was new again.

And as an older son working hard to become someone I already was, the Father did not withhold His goodness until I became good and holy enough. He filled me with His love and gave me new eyes to see Him, myself, and others through the lens of love.

When you realize who you are and know that there is absolutely nothing left to do to be loved by the Father, your life will feel new again.

That's exactly why the Father sent His Son into the world—to make life new again.

And this is not just a spiritual renewal; it is a restoration of all things, a new Heaven and a new earth, a return of creation into the love of the perfect family. God redeemed people from every tribe, tongue, and nation in this world in love and for love.

He was not content simply to tell of His love from Heaven and call people into it. He came as love in the flesh so we could see it, receive it, become it, and release it into the lives of everyone around us.

Notes

1. Genesis 33:10. You can read the whole story of Jacob's life in Genesis 25:20–33:20.

2. Matthew's genealogy (1:1–17) begins with Abraham and goes up to Jesus. Luke's genealogy (3:23–38) starts with Jesus and works back all the way to God begetting Adam.

3. The story of the prodigal son is found in Luke 15:11–32.

REFLECTING ON SECTION 1

Questions to Think and Pray Through

- Is it difficult to see yourself as God's happy thought? Why or why not? Why is it important to know that you exist because of love—that your life is a result of Papa God's perfect love?

- Have you ever thought about who you were before the foundation of the world—the person God had in mind when He looked ahead and saw you? How might this knowledge shape your identity? Why is it important to look back to the love before time in order to understand who you really are?

- Which experience can you relate to most easily— the story of the prodigal son who ran away from his father's love or the story of the diligent son who kept trying to earn his father's love? Why?

- In what ways have you tried to "build a tower" or make a name for yourself? How have your decisions in life demonstrated an orphan heart or a love vacuum—an effort to fill your heart with the love God has already promised you?

- Have you noticed many differences between your identity as you see it and your identity as God would see it? What are they? What do you need to do or believe in order to bring your thoughts more in line with how God sees you?

Prayer

Mentally let go of any motivation to fill your own heart with self-effort and the world's accomplishments and possessions. Then ask God to fill you with His love—to fill in every crack and crevice of love deficiency in your innermost being. Pray to see your identity through His eyes. Ask Him to give you encounters with His love and help you steward the birthing processes that are coming.

Vision Exercise

Frequently and confidently envision yourself as a perfectly loved child in the arms of your Father.

Next Step

Read again the section in chapter 5 on preparing your heart for an encounter with Papa's love. Go ahead and work these suggestions into your daily times of prayer. If there are any practical steps you need to take to make time for encounters with God, plan them into your schedule at least weekly.

IN

Love became human.

Theologians call this the incarnation—the in-the-flesh God, the beloved Son in the divine family stepping out of that heavenly environment into His broken creation.

Have you ever wanted to know what God looks like? This is the perfect picture.

The Son is the exact representation of the nature and the heart of the Father. (See Hebrews 1:3.) Whatever we need to learn about God, and whatever we need to experience from Him, is expressed in Jesus.

Jesus made these same claims about Himself: *"He who has seen Me has seen the Father"* (John 14:9).

Adam and Eve were sent away from Eden, and ever since that time, human beings have longed for a taste or glimpse of Heaven. Sometimes we do get those tastes and glimpses. God has made Himself known in various times and places. (See Hebrews 1:1.)

But Jesus did not come to give us just a taste of Heaven, or even only to take us there one day. He came to bring Heaven to earth.

That is the whole point of the incarnation, and it is also the whole reason we have been given His Spirit and are being conformed to His image.

This is not about escaping earth in order to go to Heaven, even though Heaven is our ultimate destination. This about bringing Heaven to earth—love in the flesh right in front of our eyes, the restoration of all that was lost or broken, the glory of God as far as we can see. That is where this whole story is going.

Jesus is Immanuel, God with us, the foretaste of Heaven on earth (see Isaiah 7:14; Matthew 1:23), or as John put it in his Gospel, *"The Word* [Jesus] *became flesh and tabernacled among us"* (John 1:14 TLV).

That is not an expression we normally use, so maybe it would help to explain what this is supposed to mean.

The tabernacle was the movable tent of worship used by the Israelites after they left Egypt in the exodus. God instructed Moses and some of the artisans and leaders to construct this tent and carry it with them in the wilderness. It was a predecessor of the temple that would be built much later.

This was the place where God's people would meet with Him, where people could know He was present, where priests would minister and encounter God in the holy of holies. It was a house for the ark of the covenant, which represented God's presence among them and was sprinkled with the blood of sacrifices.

The people brought their offerings and sacrifices for sin to the tabernacle. The cloud of God's presence descended on the tabernacle when God was speaking with Moses face to face. (See Exodus 33:11.) Joshua stayed there to keep soaking in God's presence even after Moses had left. Everything about the tabernacle was designed for the presence of Papa God.

Every time God led Israel to a new campsite in the wilderness, they packed up the tabernacle and carried it with them, just as He had instructed. This was their ongoing connection with the love and presence of the Father.

So when John says Jesus came and *"tabernacled among us"*—most English translations say only that He *"dwelt among us"* because the idea of a tabernacle is not expressed very easily with a word or two—he was giving us a very profound, loaded visual picture.

He was telling us that we meet God, see God, and hear God in Jesus. Just as Adam looked in the face of the Father when the Spirit first breathed into him, we can look into the face of Jesus and see the Father. And as we will later see, we can experience the same Spirit being breathed into us.

The perfect image and presence of God are right there for us to encounter. The divine love of the perfect family that existed before time is made visible in human flesh.

John and the other disciples were eyewitness to this God in the flesh; they *"beheld His glory…full of grace and truth"* (John 1:14).

But beholding His glory was not just for that one generation. This is the reason John and other witnesses wrote the Gospels. Through their words, and through the invitation that their words give us, we get to be witnesses too. We see God in the flesh, the perfect representation of the Father's love, not only in the stories they tell but also in God's ongoing presence in the world.

Many people embraced this love right away. Many others did not. John says that Papa God's own people that He had chosen did not recognize this divine love and rejected Him.

Still, we know that the thread of love continued. Even though human beings once again turned their face from God, He continued to turn His face toward us.

The in-the-flesh appearance of Heaven's love is the centerpiece of history and marks a turning point in God's ultimate purpose for this world: to fill the earth with His offspring who bear His image and represent His love.

He came *in* the world, *in* the mess, *in* the trials and struggles of humanity, *in* the midst of human corruption, *in* the environment of fallen, broken systems and organizations and religions, and *in* human flesh.

And *into* hearts that were longing for a touch of perfect love.

CHAPTER 6

THE SEEDS OF LOVE

Once when I preached a message on the Father's love and healing the orphan spirit at a conference in Minnesota in 2006, a pastor from the Philippines and his wife, Paul and Ahlmira Yadao, came up to me afterward. The example of the older brother who had been working out in the fields to please his father really resonated with them. They said that some deep things had been uprooted and then planted within them when I had released the Father's blessing over the congregation. Then they asked if I would be their spiritual father.

That seemed like a very big request, but after we talked and prayed about it, I agreed.

When they went back to the Philippines, they knew they were totally transformed. Perfect love had taken away fear. The people in their church could see the transformation too. They realized the leader of their small movement was no longer an orphan. Instead of leading them, Paul began to father them.

I went to the Philippines later that year and met some of the members of this congregation, which was now taking on the nature of a spiritual family. Their whole mindset had changed—from the spirit of poverty to the spirit of abundance, from orphan survival to son and daughter revival. Their attitude in the past had been that there are only so many slices in the pizza, and everybody had to compete for them. But when God started to give them provision and they began to see differently, they began to dream with Him. They shared with me about the incredible freedom they were experiencing.

Paul and Ahlmira asked if I could impart to their spiritual sons and daughters the same thing I had imparted to them. We had an amazing time with four hundred people in the room. A wind came in and knocked over the speaker system. I knew angelic activity was going on. Many people experienced a baptism of love.

From that time forward, Paul and Ahlmira have raised up a whole family of love—Kingdom people having experiences with the love of God and learning to live as sons and daughters. They have become a prototype of what our ministry dreams of—the family of Heaven on earth.

What does that look like? It looks like love moving in marriages, into the children, into businesses and school systems. One professor in this congregation was so transformed that he went from being a strong supporter of the LGBT movement to being in a strong heterosexual marriage with children today. Mass healings began taking place. They experienced story after story of radical transformation and supernatural love.

I eventually began taking Paul with me to the Middle East, South Asia, Africa, and many other parts of the world. He got a vision of how love can change nations. I watched him minister in India once, fearless in the face of opposition, and the love that was on him brought many signs and wonders into the lives of the people there.

Paul has seen how the seeds of perfect, supernatural love have transformed him, his marriage and family, his church, and even nations. What he has seen in the Philippines is a true generational move of God's Spirit in every sphere of society.

The seeds of love have grown into trees of love that are bearing the fruit of love.

This is what seeds from God do, which takes us all the way back to His words at the beginning of the human story.

Right after the fall, God made a promise about "the seed of the woman."

With our modern understanding of biology, we do not use that term. But this is a very effective image because it focuses on the contrast between the first seed of love and the seeds of deception the enemy sowed in Eden. It also points to the supernatural birth of Immanuel, and it hints at the way God continues to plant His love in the soil of this world.

The seed of the woman was a promise. That's what love does. It makes a commitment. It does not follow up a tragedy or a failure only with a rebuke. It brings hope.

The seed of the woman was also a process—a very, very long one.

God did not fix things right away. He let history play out over thousands of years. He wove the thread of love through the lives of His people in generation after generation. He waited for *"the fullness of time,"* when He *"sent forth His Son, born of a woman, born under the law, to redeem those who were under the law, that we might receive the adoption as sons"* (Galatians 4:4–5).

Do you see the values of the perfect family here?

God made a promise to the woman and her seed: they would overcome the seeds of deception, destruction, and disappointment. He promised that love would win.

Papa God worked His love and His promises into the generations of His family on earth.

When the right time came, He sent not just a Savior but a Son—through a woman, a daughter of Eve, who opened her heart to the seeds of heavenly love.

This Son grew in wisdom and stature, in obedience to His earthly parents and His heavenly Father. He entered into a process, like all seeds of love do. He waited patiently. Seasons came and went. Moments of opportunity and divine appointment opened up.

And one day, He was revealed with His perfect family from above.

The Baptism of Love

We will go back to the first seasons of this seed of love in a moment, but first I want us to look ahead to some of the fruitfulness of this seed in my life and in our times.

Before 2000, I knew in my mind that I was loved by God. Like most Christians, I had that theology. I had read it in Scripture. I had preached it to congregations. I had even experienced examples of God's love from other people.

If anyone had asked me about the Father's love, I could have told them all about it. I would have assured them that the Father loves everyone because this is His nature. I would have quoted verses about how He loved the world so much that He sent His only Son. I had no doubt that the Father's love was real.

But I had not *known* the Father's love. Not deep in my heart anyway. Not in a way that would transform me and bring me forever into the warmth, acceptance, and affirmation of the divine family's living room. Not so thoroughly that I knew beyond the shadow of a doubt that I was God's beloved son.

Theologically, I was a son. Emotionally, I was still living as an orphan.

My heart still was not satisfied. I was still working very hard in order to become someone. I was trying to earn the Father's pleasure. I wanted to be somebody in God's Kingdom. I was not convinced that I already was somebody.

I believe very many Christians can relate to that situation. But like me, they may be so convinced of the theology of the love of God that they have not noticed some of the ways they have been missing it in their experience.

I didn't know I was living from an orphan heart until that moment I was laying on the floor and hearing the Father call me His beloved son.

That happened in 2000 when I went to a small gathering in Florida. Somebody prayed for me with a really surprising prayer: "Holy Spirit, come take away anything in Leif's life that isn't comfortable with love."

Not comfortable with love? That caught me off guard a little bit. I had no idea how true it was. Then the worship leader called me up to the front. "Leif, this is the Father's song for you," he said. As he started playing, I felt the Father's presence come over me. It was like liquid love flowing through me, first just a trickle but soon a waterfall. I went down to the floor and felt waves and waves of love rolling over me and through me as I lay there. Images from my childhood came to mind—many experiences that had wounded me and scarred me—and I could feel the Father's touch healing me from all the pain and rejection that my heart had been holding onto for years.

Everything in me that had made me feel like an orphan melted away.

Everything in me that was uncomfortable with love became comfortable with love.

This stoic Norwegian was overcome with emotion as the Father's love washed over him.

When I finally got up from the floor—I was there for a long time—I had no doubt that I was a son, not an orphan. My spirit and emotions supernaturally and immediately caught up with my theology.

I even heard the Father's voice audibly—the only time I can say that has happened—"Leif, you are My son in whom I am well pleased."

Beautiful words. I will never forget them.

I had been burned out, tired out, and feeling left out. I was struggling with rejection. I had been a pastor and had started a missions organization. But I was like the prodigal son's older brother—living *for* God because I didn't know how to live *from* Him.

I was hungry and thirsty, and I didn't know why.

God knew. He had known since before the foundation of the world. He already knew the thread of perfect love woven throughout history would be woven into my life on that day. I got up from the floor as someone who was forever changed. I have no words to describe that experience other than calling it my baptism of love.

Many people have never heard of a baptism of love. Christians have talked a lot about a baptism of repentance and baptism in water. Over the last century, the idea of a baptism in the Spirit has reemerged and become increasingly recognized.

But a baptism of love? Where is that in Scripture?

It is there. The seed of the woman, the Word who became flesh and tabernacled among us, the perfect image of God who grew up as a Son, experienced a baptism of love.

I think one reason many people have not recognized this baptism is that it is part of the story of Jesus's baptism where water and the Spirit are easier to see. So let's go back to that story of how the seed of love was revealed together with His whole heavenly family one day.

At the beginning of His public ministry, Jesus came to John the Baptist to be baptized in the Jordan River. This is a familiar story, and right away we recognize the baptism in water. It is plain to see because that was what John had been doing—baptizing people in the waters of the Jordan River.

It is just as easy to recognize the baptism in the Spirit there, even if not everyone describes it that way. The Spirit appeared right after Jesus came out of the water when the dove came down and rested on Him, and He comes in on different occasions in Acts in the experience of many people who received Him.

As far as most people think about it, the baptism of Jesus has just those two elements—the water and the Spirit. Many Christians even debate whether a simultaneous baptism of water and the Spirit, as Jesus experienced, is normal for everyone who comes to faith in Him. How these things happen in sequence can be a little controversial, but a water baptism and a Spirit baptism are both biblical.[1] Not many people would disagree with that.

But another aspect of baptism comes right after Jesus came out of the water and the Spirit descended upon Him. We see the water and the dove as part of the baptism, but many people consider the Father's words to be a commentary on what was happening—something spoken about the event rather than as a third aspect of the event itself.

When the Father spoke over Jesus, He was not just commenting on what had happened. He was continuing the baptism experience. He was immersing the Son in the Father's love.

This is My beloved Son, in whom I am well pleased (Matthew 3:17).

This is an identity statement. It is the ultimate assurance that the Son would never need to build a tower for His own purposes and try to make a name for Himself.

Look at all that this statement includes:

- My—belonging to the Father
- Beloved—fully accepted, affirmed, loved
- Son—a member of the divine family, where love flourished before time began

These were the words I heard from the Father as I lay on the floor being washed in waves and waves of His love. I had already been baptized in water many years before. A few years after that, I had a dramatic baptism in the Spirit and had ministered in His power, seeing people saved, healed, and delivered in many places around the world. These were both part of my experience. But my baptism in love did something different.

Something deep inside me changed when love moved in. I knew my Papa delighted in me. I knew I was His happy thought. I felt His pleasure. I could look into His face and see Him smile. I could call out to Him, "Papa!"

I began seeing myself the way this loving Father saw me. I began seeing other people the way the Father saw them.

Papa God's perfect love took away all my fear. I was no longer afraid of rejection and no longer felt insecure. I did not feel as if I needed to strive for approval or affirmation anymore. I did not have a need to make a name for myself.

I come from a very stoic people. Norwegians typically do not go around hugging people. But I started to hug people every-where—all over the world.

I had received love. I wanted to become love. And I wanted to release love any way I could.

This was not the end of my journey of love, of course. In many ways, this was just the beginning—that birthing part of the process we've been talking about. Everything began to change.

My wife and family noticed the change. They asked me what had happened to me. My wife told me that even though I had been baptized in the Spirit and seen signs and wonders, this was very different. "This has changed you more than anything

I have ever seen in your life," she told me. I think she was very happy about it. The Father's love completely transformed me.

When Love Gets Tested

You will need to remember that this is a process. No story about a baby ends with the birthing, does it? So it is very important to be patient.

If you are a seed growing into a tree, you know this is not going to happen overnight. Your new nature has to mature. You will probably see some immediate growth and fruit, but much more is coming. If a birthing moment has not already come, it is on the way. It will happen, and then you will go through more process. And then maybe more birthing moments as the seed of love grows within you.

You will also encounter many tests along the way. You probably are aware of that. You have experienced tests in every area of growth in your life, and this one is no different.

So if you need encouragement, look at some of the biblical characters whose wonderful, enormous fruit came only after intense times of testing.

Joseph eventually made it into Pharaoh's court to live out his calling, but first he had to endure a test in the palace, a test in his purity, a test in his prison, and a test with his prophecies. It was a very long story with many setbacks, but all of the setbacks were leading him toward his destiny.[2]

Moses eventually delivered God's people from slavery and made it to the edge of the Promised Land, but he had to pass several tests first: to get to the end of himself before even starting, to put up with a lot of resistance and complaining and rebellion, to train an entire generation in the ways of faith, and to endure years in a harsh wilderness.

David eventually got to the throne, but he had to learn many lessons as a shepherd, overcome an intimidating giant, elude an irrational king, hide in a cave, and fight to restore some devastating losses.

These things can take years.

Why Did Jesus Need a Baptism of Love?

I have gone into some of the darkest places in the world and seen multitudes saved, healed, and delivered. A lot of people want to go where I've gone and have the kind of fruit I've experienced. I love seeing that desire in people, and I want them to experience those things too. The fruit of love is very beautiful and satisfying.

But it is also very costly. Many of these people who seek the fruit are not aware of the processes along the way—the sacrifices, the trials, the hardships, the disappointments, the seasons of pain.

Is the journey of love worth it? Absolutely.

Is it all pleasure and ease? Not at all.

And that is why I believe Jesus needed His baptism of love.

He endured so much. The costs of His ministry were high. The trials He went through were probably exhausting. He was contested every step of the way.

But I don't think Jesus was ever insecure or lived in fear because He was saturated in Papa God's love. I don't think He struggled with discouragement and disappointment. But He did need the testimony and validation of His Father's voice.

Jesus's baptism in the Holy Spirit was given for a ministry of power. But I believe His baptism in love was given to endure the demonic and physical attacks He would face. He needed more than integrity during His temptations in the wilderness, more than the assurance of being righteous, more than His anointing in power. He needed Papa God's affirmation of being completely, unconditionally loved.

Do you know what it's like to go through trials, struggles, adversity, pain, and disappointment without an absolute assurance of the Father's love? If you do, you know the kinds of fears and insecurities these challenges stir up. Those hardships just feed an orphan heart. Without that foundation of being immersed in love, every hardship raises very disturbing and unsettling questions: Am I in trouble? Am I being judged? Is God okay with me?

If you have the awareness that you are completely covered with Papa God's love, all of those questions are already answered.

A baptism in love is the most important requirement for success in life and ministry.

I spent many years of life and ministry knowing perfect love in my mind without knowing it in my heart. I know the questions that come up. I know the burnout that can happen. I needed to know how unrelenting, unconditional, and unfathomable the Father's perfect love is—and that it was for me.

The Father loves us more than we can imagine. His love cannot be stopped. It does not change with the seasons. It does not rise and fall with our good works and sins, our good days and bad days, or our memories and moods.

We never have to strive for it. In fact, we can't. This cannot be earned, only received.

But because this experience of unconditional love goes against our natural instincts, most Christians live life backward—in reverse of the Son.

First, we spend our lives on the cross wondering why God has forsaken us.

Then we go to the Garden of Gethsemane in deep, intense prayer, entering into a long, hard life of dealing with sickness and demonic activity.

Finally, we realize who we are and discover that our righteousness accounted for nothing in God's eyes because He had already considered us righteous by faith.

We spend years trying to enter into the Father's love.

To put this another way, we spend so much of our lives trying to step into our identity rather than stepping into our identity at the beginning and then living from that identity. We live *toward* the Father's love rather than living *from* the Father's love.

We see a completely different order in the life and ministry of Jesus.

In Jesus, the first revelation is the Father's love. This is our strength for the life of faith.

Then comes ministry and fruitfulness in the power of the Spirit.

And with that as our foundation, we can endure whatever cross we have been called to carry. We do not let fear, insecurity, or shame influence us because we know who we are, and we are secure in the Father's love.

Did you notice that Jesus received the perfect love of the Father *before* He had done any works of ministry? He got an A-plus on His report card before He had accomplished anything. At the very beginning, He had already heard a "well done."

The Father could have said many different things at Jesus's baptism: "This is the King." "This is the Savior." "This is the Anointed One." Instead, Papa God declared His love for Jesus. That speaks volumes about Heaven's priorities.

It also tells us God's template for our lives. Through faith in the Son, by entering into this perfect family's love through adoption as sons and daughters, we are completely, forever loved. We have an A-plus on our report cards before we ever take a test. We no longer live *for* love; we live *from* love.

Our orphan hearts are healed.

I know what you might be thinking at this moment. *What if I have not had this experience? If this is the Father's heart for us, why aren't more of us being filled with that kind of love?*

We will get to that. The encounter with perfect love is wonderful, but it does not happen the same way for everybody, and it is not the whole story. There is a process, there is a way to live out your hunger for this love, and God has different ways of expressing it.

For now, just focus on the main thing: to know that this is God's desire, this love is true, and it is available to you.

This is why the Word became flesh.

Notes

1. Water baptism is identified in this story of Jesus and many other places in Scripture. It's a common Christian experience. The terminology of a baptism in the Spirit was used by Jesus in Matthew 3:11 and referred to in Acts 1:5 and 11:16.

2. The main part of Joseph's journey from dream to fulfillment is found in Genesis 39–46.

CHAPTER 7

SEEDS, SOILS, AND THE GARDEN OF YOUR HEART

Let's go back to the Gospel of John for a moment.

"In the beginning was the Word," it begins. *"The Word was with God, and the Word was God"* (John 1:1).

If the Word is God, and if God is love, then the Word is love. This is a logical equation.

So the Word was the seed of love, and He was there at the very beginning.

We saw earlier that love was behind this creation. But when humanity rebelled and creation fell, this seed of love was still there—sown into the world in direct opposition to the seeds of deception sown in Eden.

Those seeds that the enemy sowed into human hearts turned us away from the Father's love. This seed in the flesh turns us back to it.

It is fascinating to see how seeds show up in the teaching and ministry of Jesus, who Himself is the seed of love.

Jesus once told a parable that He said would unlock all the other parables. If I were a disciple at the time, my antenna would have gone up immediately. A key to understanding all of them? That would be a valuable piece of wisdom.

The disciples asked Jesus to explain this parable, and He told them that if they did not understand this one, they would not understand the others. They didn't just need the information in this story; they needed to let it sink into their hearts. If it did, revelation would open up to them.

The parable was about a man who sowed seeds into a field with different kinds of soil.[1] Some of the seed fell by the side and birds ate it. Some fell in rocky places and could not grow roots in the thin soil. Some fell in the thorns and got choked as they grew. Only the seed that fell on good, deep, rich soil grew up and flourished.

These soils represent human hearts. Some receive truth, and some do not. Some read the Bible or hear the Word and immediately respond, but they don't hold it close and let it grow. Some want to grow but do not do what it takes to nourish the seed that has been planted within them.

In Jesus's parable, the initial response is not the issue. The big question is what happens after the initial response—the persistence in the process. Some people hunger and thirst for the growth of the seed and go after it. The real issue is what a person does with truth and love in the long run.

Do you see how this might be a key to all other parables and teachings? This is about receptivity and responsiveness, not just in the moment but over the course of a lifetime. And receptiveness and responsiveness open up greater revelation.

And do you see how it might be a key to receiving the seed of perfect love? An encounter is wonderful and beautiful, but by itself it is not enough. It does not solve everything. That seed needs to be nourished over time—pursued, prayed for, embraced, fed, fertilized, watered, and stewarded into maturity and fruitfulness.

There's a big difference between an encounter and a seed. A seed is necessary for a tree to grow, but just planting a seed will not guarantee a tree. An encounter like my baptism of love can be radically transforming, but by itself, it does not translate into lasting change. Some kind of stewardship and ongoing pursuit needs to happen afterward.

It is very possible to have a powerful experience—like Jacob did when he saw angels ascending and descending on a ladder from Heaven—and still have an orphan heart that never gets filled up.

If God gives you an encounter, you have a landmark event, a healing touch from Heaven, and a wonderful memory to anchor yourself in as you begin or continue your process of growing into perfect, supernatural love.

But if God plants a seed in you, and if your heart receives it freely and nourishes it over time—if you let the roots of it grow deep—your capacity to love expands, your fruit grows, and your love will be much greater in the long run. And when you have that encounter, that birthing moment, you will know what to do with it.

So your initial experience with this kind of love might look like a dramatic encounter. It might be more subtle or unfold more slowly. It might look like something in between.

This is really important to understand. Many Christians are looking for an encounter, and I will never discourage that. I know the power of that experience. Encounters with Papa's love have been a huge part of my life, and I would not trade them for anything. I want you to have them too.

But receiving supernatural love is more than just a birthing experience.

The key is not to live from encounter to encounter but to create an environment that can receive love—an atmosphere free of worry, anxiety, fear, guilt, insecurity, shame, condemnation, regret, disappointment, and everything else that interferes with love. An encounter can help with that, but it cannot maintain it.

It is up to you to prepare the soil of your heart.

What kind of soil do you have?

Everything in God's Kingdom involves the heart.

Kingdom matters are heart matters.

So when the seed of love goes into your heart, what happens to it then? Is the soil ready? Will it grow into a beautiful tree of love? Will it bear the beautiful fruit of love?

The soil of your heart determines whether other people will ever be able to taste the fruit of love that grows from the seed planted in you.

Scripture says we have been given an incorruptible seed (see 1 Peter 1:23)—the Word, Jesus, the impartation of perfect love from the Father. He is the seed that has been planted in our hearts, and when God immerses us in supernatural love, He is not giving us something new. He is uncovering what He put in us when we believed, unveiling the reality of the perfect love of the Father that was always ours.

Let that sink in for just a moment. The perfect, eternal, supernatural love of the divine, heavenly family is already in you.

You are already God's beloved son or daughter in whom He is well pleased.

The love you were created to experience and designed to represent is yours.

Note

1. You can read the whole parable and Jesus's explanation of it in Matthew 13:3–23.

CHAPTER 8

FROM ORPHAN TO AMBASSADOR

I was leading a healing school with Randy Clark and Bill Johnson in Southampton, England, in 2010. I hoped Bill's assistant Judy Franklin was going to be there. I had heard about one of my spiritual sons having an amazing experience of being set free when Judy prayed for him—a face-to-face encounter with Papa God—and I wanted to experience that too.

As it turns out, Judy was there, and I asked Bill if she could spend a little time praying for me. So she and I were able to get away from the event for a few moments. Judy asked me to close my eyes and imagine myself going on a pathway toward a wall with a big door. "Can you see it?" she asked.

"Yes, I can see it." With my Baptist background, I would call this "sanctified imagination," but it is still very clear, even all these years later. I could see a big, wooden door with a handle and a lock on it.

I had to open the door with a special kind of key, and when I went through it, I entered a gorgeous area with a waterfall, a big lake, and beautiful trees on the other side. I followed the path and saw next to the lake a bench with no one sitting on it, so I went over to it and sat down. I was overwhelmed by the surroundings and the sense of presence—peaceful, beautiful, like Heaven on earth.

Somebody came and sat with me on the bench, and at first I did not know who it was. But then I could sense that it was Jesus, even though I could not see His face. I could feel the light and warmth in Him.

After a moment He said, "What is the question that you have?"

As soon as He said it, my mind went to many different questions I could ask about things that had happened in the past. Why did I have that car accident? What about my broken neck? What about my tumor? Why didn't I get healed when I prayed for healing? Why did my recovery take so long? My mind was rambling. But I did not say anything yet.

After all of these thoughts settled down, I looked at Him and asked, "Do I really love You?"

I already knew He loved me. I did not need to ask that. But this is the question that came to mind. I had not been thinking about it before, as far as I can remember, but suddenly I wondered if my love for Him was real.

He did not answer me. He made a gesture like He was about to laugh and then disappeared.

The next moment I was back in the room with Judy, soaking wet with tears.

"What happened?" I asked. "This was more than just my imagination."

And she began describing what had happened to me. She told me I was sitting on a bench, that Jesus came in, and many other details about the scene that were going on in my thoughts.

"How do you know these things?" I asked her.

"I went up there with you. I was watching. I kept my distance." And then she said, "You are going to know that this was God."

I still had questions. I went to a Baptist college and seminary, and I had a little bit of the Thomas syndrome going on in my mind—doubts about whether this was real. I have seen a lot of things before. I had even had my baptism of love and felt waves of Papa's love flowing over me and through me. But this was stranger than that. I knew it was an encounter, but I was still trying to process it.

Then Judy made a prophetic statement: "You are an apostle of love, and the world will know it within five years. You will be known as an ambassador of love."

That sounded good to me, but I was not sure how it would happen. We went back into the conference events. I spoke that Saturday, and then I returned home.

Not long afterward, I traveled to a Muslim country I had visited many times before. I was supposed to do a five-minute speech about interfaith peace and harmony at an event where four hundred imams were attending. One of the imams, a key leader, was looking at me. He walked across the room and said, "You are the ambassador of love."

I had never heard anybody use that title apart from Judy's word to me. This was not something I had ever heard in their culture or that could be expected from their normal language. I could not have imagined a Muslim imam saying it to anyone.

At the next event I attended, something similar happened. I was at a very big mosque in a major city in this country, and many government leaders were in attendance. As I was about to speak, I was introduced as the ambassador of love. I had never done anything to promote this term. I am not sure if I had ever even repeated it outside my close circles of family and friends. But through the influential people at this mosque who heard me being introduced with this title, it began to spread.

Judy was right. Within five years, I was known in many places around the world as an ambassador of love. One encounter led to a process that worked out in many ways in many different places.

What Does an Ambassador of Love Look Like?

The Son of God became one of us so that the people who love Him could become like Him. We will explore that much more in the last section, but I want to share a few examples of how I have seen that play out in my own life. I think they will be helpful pictures of the power of supernatural love.

Once when I was visiting an Islamic university in the Middle East, I met a brilliant Muslim scholar who is very well known in that world. I was excited when I found out I could meet with him, but I realized I did not have a gift to give him. I wanted to honor him with something tangible.

I think that is very important, not only because it is appropriate within that culture, but because honor is what love looks like. I had not known ahead of time that I was going to meet with him and had not prepared. I did not have a way to show my affection toward him.

I asked my coordinator if he had a copy of one of my books, *Seeing Through Heaven's Eyes*. Fortunately, he did. I wrapped it up and gave it to this scholar when we met, and he expressed great appreciation for it.

About two days later, I was getting ready to leave that country when my coordinator got a call from this man.

"I don't know what has happened," he said. "I started to read the book last night, and then something that feels like waves has been coming over me. I do not normally cry, but I have not been able to stop crying. Every time I open the book, this occurs. What is happening to me?"

I got to meet this scholar again about a year later. He still could not describe what had happened to him over the last year, but I understood. He was being changed from the inside out.

This was not just a private transformation in his own life. Other imams and clergy around him could see the change that had taken place and were being affected too. I could see a shift in the environment. The spiritual temperature changed. He had accidentally bumped into the baptism of love.

I had another experience with another influential Muslim leader back in my office in the United States. I had recently returned from England and then went to Washington, DC, for an event related to the Freedom Act near the end of President Barack Obama's second term. This leader was also at the event, and when it ended, he said he wanted to visit my home.

So we returned to Atlanta together. We went to a mosque together, and then we met in my office. I had done a little preparation before he came by putting the Quran and the Bible on the highest shelf in my office. While we were seated in my office, he stood up and took the Quran off the shelf, then sat back down in a chair and began to read it in Arabic. I was still jet-lagged and about to fall asleep, but I tried to straighten up and keep my eyes open.

The next moment, I could feel the presence of Jesus coming into the room. I have to admit that I was thinking, *This is not a good time, God.* But it got heavier, and I was feeling a little under the influence of the Spirit. I am sure that I must have looked drunk when I was looking at him. And the presence just kept getting thicker and thicker.

"What are you doing to me?" he asked.

"What do you mean?"

"What is this tingling? It is going from my head all the way down into my feet, up and down like waves. What is this?"

"Oh," I said, "That's just the presence of Jesus. He is pouring His love over you. Can I pray for you?" I had enough favor to pray for him, but not to actually touch him, so I went over to him, put my hand a few inches over his head, and prayed. To me, it felt like heat was going down into his stomach area and making circles like fire and then disappearing.

The next morning, I went to his hotel to pick him up. I was going to open my car door for him, but he said very firmly, "No, I want you to come in here—up to my room." He had a beautiful, long beard and warm, brown eyes, but his voice was a little bit strict.

This was very unusual. Whenever I have been in the Middle East, I would not go to an imam's or scholar's room. Was I in trouble? I did not know what he had in mind. It felt very awkward.

When I walked into his room, he went over to his laptop where his whole family was on Skype—two wives, children of all ages. "I want you to give them what I received yesterday."

So I prayed over Skype, and the presence of Jesus filled that room in the Middle East where his family was gathered. They had encounters with divine love, and those encounters have transformed their lives.

When this man returned to his home country, he began to notice things he never had before: people living in poverty, beggars, people in pain, women who could not get pregnant. These people had been there all along—he had grown up with this pain all around him—but the common attitude is that Allah is going to do whatever Allah is going to do. He had not noticed these things before he was filled with a heart of love.

But now, with the heart and the eyes of love, he saw brokenness. I don't know if he had prayed a salvation prayer yet, but he was being changed by this love from the inside out. He had new lenses on his eyes. He was beginning to see what Jesus sees, feel what Jesus feels, and say what Jesus says without realizing that a seed of love had been planted in him. He had begun to feel love that he had never known before.

This experience eventually led to a healing meeting in a mosque. He wanted to address the brokenness. But he did not know what to do, so he called me. "Can you help me? I do not know how to pray that way." So I offered to help. I have actually been to that mosque now to do a healing meeting.

It has been amazing to see what has happened in this man's life. His son has started feeling the same things and seeing with eyes of compassion. He began to recognize the pain of girls who could not be educated, some of whom had been abused, so he opened up a school for them. I cut the ribbon for it. It was amazing.

God had once told me that He was going to take me to some of the darkest places in the world so that people would know that we can overcome evil with good and that the goodness of God leads to repentance. He has been true to that word.

I recently received a national peace award from the president of a large Islamic country. How do you go from being a broken, suicidal addict to an honoree in an Islamic republic who is known for his love? Only God can do that. And when this president handed me the plaque, it had words on it that only God could orchestrate: "To Leif Hetland, Ambassador of Love."

Again, these are words that I have never promoted and were only told to me in a private prophetic declaration. Now I have been introduced with that title by grand imams of royal mosques, on TV in a Muslim-majority country, and in meetings with the Muslim leadership of large nations.

I have never used that title for myself, but my Papa is the King. I get to represent Heaven on earth. I know the culture I am coming from—that perfect environment in the family of Heaven—and I have learned its language.

And the seed has grown in me so that I can describe it in such a way that blind eyes can see and deaf ears can hear it.

Where It Begins

You will read about more examples in the next section of this book, but they all begin the same way: an incarnation. The seed of love that brings encounters with love creates people who love. We receive love, give love, become love, and release love.

If we are going to bring the love of Heaven into this earthly realm, we need to be immersed in that love ourselves. We need to know we have an A-plus on our report card before we go out and complete our assignments.

We need to look into the darkest places of this world and see them with the eyes of love.

Jesus became an incarnation of love so we could become an incarnation of love. That new identity first appears in our homes, families, neighborhoods, and workplaces. But we can live it out anywhere.

It all depends on what kind of soil is in our hearts and how we steward the seed of love that has been planted within us.

CHAPTER 9

THE JOURNEY OF LOVE

Once when I was ministering in Norway, a very frustrated man came up to talk to me. "You prayed for a baptism of love last time I was here. The opposite is happening!"

He explained that he was having more trouble with anger and fear. His wife had noticed too, and she didn't like what she was seeing. He wondered why things would turn in the opposite direction after a prayer for supernatural love.

Sometimes weeks or months after an impartation of love people come up and tell me how much their lives have changed. But sometimes I sense a little frustration when things are taking some time. And I have had to learn to recognize and appreciate the times when things seem to be going in the wrong direction.

When love moves in, fear moves out because *"perfect love casts out fear"* (1 John 4:18). So the fact that bad things were manifesting on their way out was a very good sign. So I was actually excited by this man's testimony. I gave him an answer he certainly wasn't expecting. "Good!"

He looked at me like I was crazy. "What do you mean? How is that good?"

My encouragement sounded very abnormal to him, of course. His experience had really bothered him, and he thought it was very different from what ought to be happening. But think about it like this. When love starts to move in, other things start to move out. Fear comes up. Anger resurfaces. Our transformation is an inside-out process.[1]

The baptism of love was doing its work. It was uprooting the things that cannot coexist with love. When we get squeezed, whatever is inside starts to come out. That's a good thing.

Later this man had some more breakthrough because he realized he was in the first trimester of a pregnancy that would birth supernatural love.

Yes, there might be some discomfort early in that process. But—if we shift the metaphor here from pregnancy to gardening—when you plant a beautiful garden with the best seed, you want to pull the weeds out of the way. When your Father puts a seed of love in your heart, He creates a clearing, preparing for what will eventually become a beautiful tree of love.

I have prayed with and ministered to many people who had an encounter with love because they had already been going through a long process of preparation. I have prayed with and ministered to many others whose encounters started a long process of labor and birthing and nurturing.

The birth and the process go hand in hand, but not in the same order or template for everyone. And there is nothing wrong with that. This is normal. It works in different ways because Papa God knows the hearts of each of His children.

When the Word became flesh and lived among us, He entered into a process too. He grew in wisdom and stature and favor with God and man. (See Luke 2:52.) Like every human being, He grew physically, psychologically, emotionally, and spiritually. But even more, He grew in the expression of His relationship with the Father.

When He was twelve years old, He and His parents went to Jerusalem for Passover, and on the way back, His parents realized He was not in the traveling party.

Can you imagine what that must have felt like? God had given them one of the most important missions a parent could ever have—to watch over the Son of God on earth. And they lost Him! Of course, when God is doing such an important work, He is going to be watching over the process. I'm sure they took some comfort in that.

Immediately, they went back to Jerusalem and looked for Him for three days. Where did they find Him? In His Father's house—the temple.

Do you remember how John described the incarnation? *"The Word became flesh and **tabernacled** among us"* (John 1:14 TLV). To update the language a little more with a word that has the same meaning, He *templed* among us.

The human temple of God was found sitting in the stone temple of God.

The person of presence was hanging out in the place of presence.

And it should not surprise us that all the religious leaders listening to His questions were astonished at how much understanding He had. (See Luke 2:41–50.)

Scripture gives us some pictures like this of Love in the flesh making a powerful impression. But we have to remember that He was at least thirty when He had that threefold baptism experience in water, the Holy Spirit, and perfect love. He had not yet begun His public ministry. What were all the other days like in those thirty years leading up to it?

Imagine perfect love in day-to-day life, in the ordinary experiences on Mondays and cloudy days and dark nights. Imagine the carpentry that went on in His earthly father's workshop, or what must have happened if His mother ran out of olive oil (did He make more?), or the reactions of the village kids He played with (did He win every game?), or even just the conversations around the dinner table.

Love did not just live among us in the mountaintop experiences of baptism and encounters with God and the noteworthy stories of the Gospels. He lived—and still lives—among us on very ordinary days.

This is one reason it's so important to value both your encounters and the times in between them. The Father is not loving you and ministering to you only during those intense, overwhelming moments. He's loving you and ministering to you while you wash the dishes or take out the garbage.

Love thrives in the ordinary.

We have that same calling. We don't just experience love that way—in the mountaintops and valleys. We live it out that way too.

When we have a dramatic encounter with God in a ministry setting, it can be a wonderful experience. But we do not stay there. We take it back into the day-to-day, the ordinary, even the mundane.

If we begin to think that God's power is with us during those spiritual highs but somehow absent in daily life, we start living from mountaintop to mountaintop and don't know what to do in the valleys.

And I have to be honest with you. A *lot* of Christians are doing that. They live for the next conference, the next encounter, or the next mountaintop moment. And they haven't yet learned how to experience Papa's love while driving to work, taking care of the kids, or unwinding at the end of the day.

I had some mountaintop moments in 2013. I knew they were going to come sometime because I had been given many prophetic words and dreams. They suddenly started coming to pass during that year, and I thought, Wow, this season has arrived!"

And God said, "Leif, look out on the horizon. Do you see that next mountaintop? I want to invite you there too." Wow, what an amazing thought. I was so encouraged. I was eager to accept that invitation. More encounters, more fulfillment, and more joy. That sounded wonderful.

And then Jesus started walking me down the mountainside. "Lord, why are we going this way?" Because the path from one mountaintop to another goes through some valleys. These are not always bad valleys or hard ones, necessarily, but they are also not the mountaintop.

Man tries to build bridges from high points to high points. God builds roads over the whole landscape, even through valleys. The path from glory to glory does not always feel like glory in between.

The glory at each end of that road is real. But going from glory to glory does not always feel glorious the whole way. Sometimes you have to go down to get to a new high. So the journey to the next mountain may involve going down into a wilderness and then starting to go up again on a new mountainside.

The point is that everybody who encountered Jesus, whether as a child or an adult, in the stories of Scripture or between the lines, in the dramatic moments and the mundane events, saw the face of love when they needed it.

Some people saw the dove come down at Jesus's baptism and the radiance of Heaven at Jesus's transfiguration. But in between, lepers saw the face of cleansing, paralytics saw the face of healing, sinners saw the face of forgiveness, parents and elders saw the face of honor and respect, the poor saw the face of generosity, and on and on we could go.

Jesus did not just receive love and show love. He was a manifestation of love. And He became the face of love for everyone who encountered Him.

And He still is, and He still does.

Note

1. Whenever something comes out of us that does not look like the fruit of the Spirit, it points to a root we don't want. The fruit reveals the root. These manifestations can happen as the root is being uprooted, but they also tell us to continue submitting those things to the baptism of love. Jesus wants them healed, not covered up. (Stockman, *Love That Baptizes Our Grief.*)

CHAPTER 10

WHAT DOES YOUR HEART REALLY BELIEVE?

Imagine growing up thinking that you were an illegitimate child born in poverty—you had few opportunities in life and always had to do without extras. You probably developed a poverty mindset in that situation, always thinking about what you were lacking rather than what you had. Over time, you became well trained in fear, insecurity, and disappointment.

What if one day you discovered that you were actually the son of a multibillionaire, and all these years, you could have had access to anything you wanted? That sounds like hitting the jackpot, doesn't it? All you have to do is say yes to your inheritance.

That's easy. Your struggles are over.

But soon you discover that sudden wealth isn't easy at all. Though your birthright makes you the heir of your father's massive holdings and enterprises, you are reluctant to take command. The people in that world don't take you seriously. You don't think you have what it takes to handle the responsibility. Your new life feels like a foreign culture.

What is the problem in this situation? Identity. The identity you have always perceived for yourself and the identity that is legally yours are many miles apart. On paper, you are a multibillionaire. In your heart, you are still a poor child from a broken home. You are believing a deeply ingrained lie because it took root in you over many years.

Jesus demonstrates for us what it looks like to believe the truth about yourself. The Father declared Him to be the beloved Son, and even though that identity was immediately tested in the wilderness, Jesus rooted His life in the Father's words.

In fact, that was Jesus's model for His entire earthly ministry. He said He only did what He saw the Father doing, and He only spoke what He heard the Father saying. (See John 5:19 and 12:49–50.) Even as a boy, He told His parents He was about His Father's business. (See Luke 2:49.) He knew who He was: the Lamb of God who takes away the sins of the world; the way, the truth and the life; the true bread from Heaven; the light of the world; the resurrection and the life; the Son of Man and Son of God.[1]

One of Jesus's disciples learned this lesson of identity very well.

All of Jesus's disciples knew He loved them, but only one kept calling himself *the disciple Jesus loved* (John 13:23 NLT).

Can you imagine what would happen if I kept referring to myself in my messages as "the speaker Jesus loves"? It would be like telling everyone, "I'm His favorite!"[2] I'm not sure it would go over very well.

But this is how John referred to himself throughout his Gospel, and he made love the central theme of his letters. John learned to love John the way Jesus loved John.

John embraced and embodied this love so thoroughly that it became his identity—the "name" he used for himself in his writing. Remember, names in the Bible are very important, rarely just names. By calling himself *the disciple Jesus loved,* he was telling everyone, "This is who I am!" That was his new identity.

This is why John was able to hear about the one who was going to betray Jesus. He was leaning against Jesus in love. (See John 13:21–26.) Those who lean close to the Lord get to hear His secrets.

This is why John was still standing at the cross after the other disciples had fled and why Jesus entrusted John to take care of His mother. John understood that the fellowship of suffering is part of a relationship of love.

And this is why John received the Revelation. With John in exile, Jesus came to him and entrusted him with this message of the future. John could handle it because he was immersed in love.

John could not have written the things he wrote—that God is love, that those who walk in love have fellowship with the Father, that loving the world's ways puts us at odds with God, that it is an amazing privilege even to be called a child of God[3]— if he had not been at rest in the Father's love. He exuded love because he was filled with love.

Identity is very important. Life changes when you know who you are. This is what we saw with Jacob too. Who you are—or who you think you are—profoundly affects the way you live. Doing always flows from being.

Do not take that the wrong way. It's easy to get these things out of balance.

At one extreme, some people focus on doing to the neglect of being. They begin to define themselves by their activities, their job, their accomplishments. At the other extreme, some people focus on being to the neglect of doing. It's all a matter of the heart, and actions really don't matter.

These are part of the same total package, two sides of the same coin. It is very true that the heart is our priority, and whatever we do flows out of who we believe we are. Identity does come first. But actions always come from identity.[4]

When we overemphasize "being," we end up leaning toward mysticism and miss the practical side of our love. When we overemphasize "doing," we end up leaning toward performance or even fanaticism and miss the relational side of our love.

We have to find a balance between those things—or, even better than balance, an integration of the two, a rhythm of life. When we harmonize them, with being and doing as two sides of the same coin, we mature in Christlikeness.

Jesus is the perfect example of this harmony. He demonstrated the complete union between being and doing. His outward behavior never contradicted His innermost being, and His innermost being never led to inconsistent behavior.

Jesus exemplified the rhythm of life.

He knew who He was and walked in the authority of His identity.

That's a great model for our lives. We are actually called to recognize who we are and then manifest our inner identity outwardly.

This is what Scripture says about Jesus. When He performed His first miracle at the wedding in Cana—a celebration where He turned water into wine—He *"manifested His glory"* (John 2:11). He demonstrated on the outside what was already on the inside.

Our calling is to manifest our glory, or rather the glory God has put within us as bearers of His image. In other words, we receive perfect, supernatural love, we become love, and then we release love. This can be challenging in some situations.

Once when I was ministering in Pakistan, an imam spread a lie about me that I had burned a Quran and blasphemed the prophet Muhammad. About five hundred men showed up with guns and knives and took over the area where we were going to have an evangelistic and healing meeting.

Everyone I worked with knew I had never done such things, but you know how slander often works. People assume the worst. So we had to cancel our event and run for our lives.

I called people back home and asked them to pray because a group of armed men were making their way toward our hotel to kill me. I got out in time, and eventually things settled down.

Love did not naturally flow out of me toward the man who stirred up that situation. I was not feeling glory on the inside.

A couple of years later, I was in a meeting with all of the top imams in Pakistan. Many of them were my friends, and I was even being honored at this event by the grand imam. As I sat there safely under the authority of this leader, I looked around the room and saw the imam who had spread lies about me. And I recognized that I had a golden opportunity to clear my reputation and embarrass this man. I had the upper hand.

I have to admit, that was very tempting. After all, this guy had destroyed a meeting that we had spent fifty thousand dollars on and months of work to prepare for. I had to run for my life and wait for the turmoil to die down. It had not been an easy situation to deal with, and it cost me a lot both emotionally and financially. I could easily have put him in his place.

Natural instincts take us in that direction. You and I both know the kinds of thoughts that come to mind when you get the chance to put an enemy in his place. But that's not what perfect love does. If you've been bathed in supernatural love, you recognize a higher way.

I realized that this situation presented me with two very different opportunities: an opportunity for retribution and an opportunity to bless. Retribution would have been satisfying—for a moment. But what would that have accomplished in the long run? Nothing very good. Blessing an enemy, though, can change the whole environment for years to come.

I don't think I could have possibly seen the situation that way if I had not already been on a journey of love. I had received love and blessing from the perfect family and was totally transformed. And I knew enough to recognize that receiving this kind of love is only the start. Once you receive it, it becomes part of you. You step into it completely, and it has to flow out of you.

I was able to embrace that man before the day was over. Neither of us said a word about what had happened two years earlier, and no one else in the room knew. But the wall of division came down, the ice melted, and fear was undone because perfect love always casts out fear.

Both of us were set free.

I still have a picture from that meeting. I'll never forget the face of this man who knew I had the authority to punish him and saw me walk in the authority of love instead.

Jesus walked in this authority all the time, without fail. His years of ministry were filled with unconditional forgiveness and love. He healed and delivered people because He looked at them with compassion.[5] He told His followers to pray for their enemies and bless them. (See Matthew 5:44.)

He set the example when He asked the Father to forgive His tormentors because they did not understand what they were doing. (See Luke 23:34.) His heart was never set on punishment or revenge. It was always about expressing the eternal love of the perfect family from before time.

He demonstrated the thread of love woven throughout history.

Where Does Your Heart Live?

Remember when we asked the question about why more people are not experiencing this kind of love? What do you do if you want your orphan heart to be healed? What do you do if you want to be like John—to know you are a disciple Jesus loves?

We've talked a bit about preparing your heart, pursuing the Father, asking to be filled with His love, and opening up to Him. This is a great posture to live in all the time.

But if you want Jesus's kind of love to sink into your heart, I would also suggest meditating on John 15. Explore the depth of that chapter. In that section of John's Gospel, Jesus is spending the evening before the crucifixion with His followers, and He is telling them all the important things they really need to remember. He knows they are about to experience a great trial and that He won't be by their side for a few days to explain things to them.

This is His big takeaway message, as if to say, "Listen, guys, above all else, you have to get this."

First, He tells them to abide in Him like branches on a vine. (See John 15:1–8.)

Most of us don't live in an agricultural society or near a vineyard, but we know enough to get this image. Branches don't have life in them unless they are connected to the vine and its roots.

That's what Jesus does for us. Connected to Him, we are rooted in eternity and able to be filled with eternal love and bear the fruit of love. Disconnected from Him, we are just branches without a lifeline.

Then Jesus explains how the impartation of love works. As the Son of God in human flesh, He received love from the Father. He expressed that love to His followers and told them to camp out in that place—to live there, saturate themselves in this love, and let it fill them like life itself.[6]

This is our inheritance—to experience the same love the Father had for Jesus and to walk in the same love Jesus had for the Father. We enter into that intimate fellowship of the heavenly family, receiving and returning the love between the Father and the Son and the Holy Spirit.

So Jesus invites His friends into that love to experience it deeply.

But it does not end there. He then tells them to love one another in the same way they had been loved by Him. (See John 15:12.)

How had He loved them? Unconditionally. Constantly. Deeply. Supernaturally.

And then Jesus describes the magnitude of His love. This is the kind of love that leads someone to lay down his life for another. (See John 15:13.)

If these followers of Jesus—actually, these friends, as He goes on to tell them—really love one another like He has loved them, they will carry a sacrificial love, a selfless love, a life-on-the-line kind of love. They will be called to seek the good of others in every situation—just like Jesus has showed them.

Paul and other New Testament writers talked about this amazing love too. In fact, Paul penned one of the greatest passages on love ever written. It's one of the best places to learn the language of love—the agape kind of love that stands above all others in its faithfulness and certainty.

Before describing this kind of love, Paul makes some pretty bold statements.

He tells them, for example, that if Christians don't have this kind of love, everything else we do is pretty much worthless. Not mediocre. Not just less than the best. Not "nice try, but let's do better." It's *"nothing"* (1 Corinthians 13:2–3).

We can preach, pray, prophesy, move mountains by faith, give to the poor, and even sacrifice our own bodies, but without love, none of that amounts to anything. (See First Corinthians 13:1–3.)

That is a challenge to every one of us who has sought more power, more signs and wonders, more fruitfulness, and more experiences more eagerly than we have sought supernatural love.

It tells us a lot about God's values and the climate of Heaven.

It also reorients our priorities. All the fruitfulness we seek in life and ministry, all the prayers we pray, all the things we want to accomplish for God and with God—all of it is futile if love is not at the center of it.

Can you imagine going through a life of service that includes attending church, giving tithes and offerings, praying for the sick, giving to the poor, receiving healing, growing in faith, and then hearing this from God: "I appreciate the effort, but that was all about you, not about love, so it doesn't count for anything"?

Granted, you probably would not do some of those things if love was not at least part of your motivation. And our motives are usually mixed anyway, with different reasons for doing what we do and love somewhere in there among the rest of them. And Papa God is gracious enough to take our hints of love and count them as something more.

But this is still a sobering thought. The things we do for God—or better, with God—have to carry the values and flavor and Spirit of God. Otherwise they don't accomplish anything lasting.

If God is love, love has to be at the center of everything.

Paul goes on to describe what this kind of love looks like:

Love suffers long and is kind; love does not envy; love does not parade itself, is not puffed up; does not behave rudely, does not seek its own, is not provoked, thinks no evil; does not rejoice in iniquity, but rejoices in the truth; bears all things, believes all things, hopes all things, endures all things. Love never fails (1 Corinthians 13:4–8).

This is the climate of love, the atmosphere of Heaven, room temperature in the company of God and His family.

I'm always amazed when I see people seeking God with all their heart but without a loving spirit. I understand this paradox; orphan hearts reaching out for the Father's love do not have much experience in their new culture. They fall back on old habits and attitudes. But love is the whole purpose. It is supposed to be the starting point, not just where we end up.

The best way to pursue the God who is love is to embrace love from the beginning. Try reading through Paul's description of love again. The picture he gives us there is what the Father is like and what Jesus demonstrated in the flesh.

The love of the heavenly family is always unselfish, always generous, always hopeful.

It keeps no records of wrong and never fails.

It never wavers, never wanes, and never becomes unreliable.

It just *is*—like God, unchanging, unbroken, invincible.

To help the nature of God's love to go deeper into your heart, read through that passage a few times substituting "Father" everywhere the text says "love."

"The Father suffers long and is kind, the Father does not envy."

"The Father bears all things, believes all things, hopes all things, endures all things."

And if you want to start declaring and counting on the kind of love God has put within you, go ahead and do the same thing, substituting "love" with "I." This is where you're headed, after all.

"I suffer long and am kind, I do not envy."

"I bear all things, believe all things, hope all things, endure all things."

This is God's purpose for you—to carry His heart within yourself, to become love just as He is love. Then, whenever you hear an impatient or rude word come out of your mouth, you can quickly remind yourself that this is not who you are. It may have been in your old nature, and it may be coming up because it's on its way out, but it's not your God-given new nature.

You begin to become the love you have received so you can then release the love you've become. Your heart is being saturated in supernatural love.

The journey of love continues.

The thread of love is being woven in and around your life, just as it has been woven in and around all of history.

This is the message Jesus is teaching in John 15. He has received love from the Father, even though He *is* love in His before-the-flesh nature. And He has become love and released love for His disciples and everyone else who comes into contact with Him.[7] Then He tells His disciples, "Okay, you see what's going on there? Go and do the same."

That's the fruitfulness that abides forever.

That's the seed that becomes a tree that becomes a forest.

That's where the journey of love is leading us.

Notes

1. The first of these is John the Baptist's declaration in John 1:29. The others, just a sampling of Jesus's identity statements, are found in John 3:17; 5:25–27; 6:35, 41, 48; 8:12, 28; 11:25; and 14:6.

2. I actually believe that I'm His favorite. But I believe you are too!

3. See First John 4:7–11; 2:15; 3:1–3.

4. James dealt with this in his letter, going so far as to claim that faith (a heart issue) without works (a behavior issue) is dead (James 2:14–26). After all, if real faith produces fruit, and no fruit ever comes from our faith, then is our faith actually real? You can have works without faith (legalism, religion, hypocrisy), but you can't have faith without works. The heart is, but the heart also does.

5. See Matthew 9:36; 14:14; 15:32; Mark 1:41; 6:34; 8:2; and others.

6. *"As the Father loved Me, I also have loved you; abide in My love"* (John 15:9).

7. I am aware that Jesus sometimes spoke very harsh words to the religiously legalistic and hard-hearted people around Him. But I believe those were still loving words—the only approach that might break down the walls of judgmentalism and hypocrisy.

CHAPTER 11

JESUS—LORD AND LOVER

Look around at today's social landscape.

Political rivalries may be more heated than we have ever seen them in our lifetime. Liberals slander conservatives; conservatives slander liberals. Online conversations are bitter and contentious, unrest over social issues such as racism and poverty have been intensifying, and many people seem to have extremely short tempers.

Culture wars are raging. These are polarizing times.

When I look around at my ethnically and religiously diverse neighbors—a Buddhist, a Muslim, several Christians—I see them wondering where the love of God is in all of this. Many people are focused on "the other side." The news commentators and political parties keep trying to show us just two options: us or them.

But someone once asked Jesus a question about love, and His answer gives us another option. Jesus was great about giving third options. Whenever someone tried to demand an either-or answer from Him, He always came up with another angle. He refused to let polarizing people push Him into one of their categories.

The context of this question about love was a conversation about the way to eternal life. The man who asked the question was able to quote two very important laws—the same laws that Jesus quoted when someone asked Him which of God's commandments was most important.

I don't know if you realize this, but not all commandments are created equal. Jesus put some commandments higher than others. When He was asked about the greatest, He quoted the Old Testament commandments to love God and to love your neighbor. He said everything else fit into one of those purposes. (See Matthew 22:34–40.)

So when someone quoted these same laws to Jesus and then asked, *"Who is my neighbor?"* Jesus took the opportunity to shift our thinking about how love is expressed in this divisive world. He told a story about unexpected mercy—a hated Samaritan selflessly loving a beaten and wounded Jew—as an example of loving your neighbor. (See Luke 10:25–37.)

Did you get that? A "neighbor" can look like the least likely candidate to give or receive love. The idea of a neighbor does not fit within our social boundaries and divisions. A neighbor is very often someone who doesn't look, talk, or believe like we do.

When we receive love from God, we stop dividing the world into categories and let go of our animosities toward everyone who doesn't fit within ours. We can love Democrats and Republicans, Muslims and Christians, rich and poor, pro-testors and traditionalists, and everyone else we meet.

We can love people this way because we have read the end of the book. It ends very well. We see a family filled with every nation, tongue, tribe, and language. God's story started with a family and will end with a family.

It began with a creation that was *"very good"* (Genesis 1:31), and it will end with a new Heaven and new earth that are even better. It began in a perfect environment of love and will end in a perfect environment of love.

We are living in the middle of the story right now, so that perfect environment can be very hard to see. But Papa God fills us with this kind of love supernaturally—the seed that grows into a mature forest of love that reveals His glory.

So we never have to choose between us and them in the way we love. We say no to the polarizing arguments that the world keeps pushing. Like Jesus, we consider the third option.

Have you ever stopped to think about that? When the world keeps giving you two choices, you are not obligated to pick one of them. No matter how often you are told to choose sides, choose the side of Jesus. Choose supernatural love. Surprising love. Honoring love.

The world sets us up for division by pitting everyone against one another. The perfect love of the divine family looks across those divisions to honor and care for people in spite of them.

Love That Looks Like Honor

If you look closely enough, you can find something to honor in everyone. Natural human love looks for something to honor in the people we like and stops looking in people who are different from us. Supernatural love keeps looking, keeps hoping, and keeps finding ways to honor others—even when those ways are hard to see. This is very important because wherever honor is, life flows. Dishonor quenches life and produces death.

Do you remember when we looked at the love before time between the Father, the Son, and the Holy Spirit? It was a perfect picture of honor. The Trinity models honor for us. The Father honors the Son and the Spirit, the Son honors the Father and the Spirit, and the Spirit honors the Father and the Son. This continuing cycle of honor creates oneness and makes life flow constantly.

This is how things operate in the Kingdom of God. It is a culture of honor. The family of Heaven and Kingdom families on earth are kept together by the superglue of honor.

Have you ever noticed how Jesus honored even those who dishonored Him? He honored His own followers too, but many of the people dishonored by society—demoniacs, tax collectors, women with bad reputations—had their honor restored by the words He spoke and the works He did. Regardless of how people looked on the outside, Jesus saw something to honor on the inside. He saw the real identity the Father had given them.

Imagine what that would look like today. Think about the political figure you can tolerate the least. Picture yourself saying, "He/she is fearfully and wonderfully made, beloved and adored, so important that Jesus died for this person. I honor this person because Jesus does."

If you have become immersed in the culture of social media, you will not be able to say this very easily. If you read those comments and have conversations about current events, you know how rare it is to hear or see words like this about a political adversary.

Imagine speaking highly about society's outcasts, blessing people who make hateful comments online, or praying for terrorists because you know that even though their acts are serving the kingdom of darkness, their souls are precious to God.

If our love does not look like honor, it cannot be a reflection of the Father's love. We need to reevaluate the source because the love of Jesus is rooted in honor.

In our current culture, where dishonor is normal, people are often surprised when they experience someone responding from a place of honor. Actually, they are surprised when they see any evidence of supernatural love.

I hope you notice that there is an opportunity in that. If supernatural love and honor are so rare, and if this kind of expression of the Father's love surprises people, then we have a greater opportunity than ever to demonstrate who God is to the world around us.

As the world seems increasingly divided, we can choose to love and honor God's way, without an agenda or hook. But our love must be more than words. When love is genuine, it's in our hearts, our words, and our actions. It looks very much like Jesus.

Love That Looks Like Jesus

Let's go back to that commandment Jesus gave His disciples the night before His crucifixion: *"Love one another as I have loved you"* (John 15:12). We often read through that statement too quickly, as if it says something like "be nice to each other."

No, look at it more closely. It tells us to love others in the same way we have been loved by God.[1] That is a radical thought.

This points to that very important principle Jesus already hinted at. He was loved by the Father and therefore expressed that love to His followers.

This is how love always works. We already have natural human love, but we cannot love with supernatural love unless we first receive it. John wrote in one of his letters, *"We love because he first loved us"* (1 John 4:19 NIV). We can only impart what we have received.

Please do not miss the magnitude of what Jesus was saying in this command to love as we have been loved.

Our souls are like a well that can only be truly filled with perfect, divine love. This divisive, contentious world often comes to drink from our wells, but instead of this perfect love, people often receive only the stagnant water of our theological arguments. This is actually just another example of worldly divisiveness. It's more of the same. So they go away thirsty.

I have found that the world is not looking for doctrine.[2] It's looking for the kind of love the Father manifested to them in human form. It's looking for Love in the flesh, the love of Immanuel that is now operating in His people.

No matter how invisible God is in His spiritual nature, He has become visible in Jesus, and Jesus is supposed to become visible in everyone who believes in Him.

Without love, it is impossible for us to see God. Without love at work within us, it is impossible for anyone else to see God in us. When we love, we open blind eyes to see something of the living God.

This is why it is so important to recognize Jesus as both Lord and Lover. This is not a contest. It's not one or the other. He's our Lord, and He's also our Lover. When we see Jesus as Lord, we see His commandment to love God and others as our highest calling to pursue at all costs. When we see Him as Lover—the embodiment of this kind of love—we see what love looks like in the flesh, which means we also see what love should look like in *our* flesh.

Remember when we talked about balance between being and doing? This calls for the same kind of balance. Just as Jesus fully integrated being and doing, He fully integrates His nature as Lord and Lover. And if we don't see Him as both—if we don't integrate those views of Him—our relationship with Him gets out of balance.

People who see Jesus only as Lover are focused on receiving His love for themselves—a great place to start, but not at all where we finish. People who see Jesus only as Lord stay in performance mode trying to please Him and might miss out on love altogether.

But Lord and Lover are in perfect harmony in Jesus. He has authority, but He loves tenderly. He is both our commander and our example. And His Spirit is the power that works within us to fill us so much that we overflow with His authoritative love.

"Follow Me"

We cannot love others beyond the capacity we have allowed God to love us.

You can try if you like, but it isn't going to work. You may be able to love pretty well, but you will not be able to love supernaturally. You can't love like Papa God does if you haven't encountered His love supernaturally.

If we have not received the Father's love, we cannot release it. So if we are going to love a hate-filled world, heal the wounded masses, touch the lepers, cherish the widows, protect the orphans, and give life to the dying, we will need to be filled with the love of God ourselves.

I'm not sure if you have noticed what this means. If you are going to love your neighbor as yourself, you are going to have to love yourself. You will have to learn to see you like the Father sees you.

This idea did not go over well in the Scandinavian culture and religious background I came from. It seems too daring and inappropriate, selfish. But think about how this works. If you do not love yourself like Papa God loves you, why would your neighbor want to be loved in the same insufficient way? In fact, you *cannot* love others with supernatural love if you have this root issue of rejection or self-hatred.

Again, you cannot give away what you do not have.

Many Christians still need to deal with a root of self-negligence or self-rejection—unhealed wounds that affect every area of life. If you're walking around with open wounds, the love God pours into you leaks out, and you can never get filled up. Letting yourself be loved by the Father is the only way you can let your love go out to others.

I know this because I would not have the love I have had for people if I had not received it myself. I've also never doubted since my baptism of love in 2000 that I am always surrounded by and filled with the love of the Father. So when I stand in a peace conference in one of these regions that the Gospel has never reached, I can give a talk as a son and release the love of Heaven. I know it's in me, and I know it comes out. The entire atmosphere can be transformed. I have never witnessed the transforming effects of love like I have in some of the darkest places of this world.

This is how we follow Jesus when He tells us to love others the way He has loved us.

Notes

1. In Matthew 5:44, Jesus also tells us to love our enemies and pray for them, so this is not just a command to love other believers, though that's where the divine family's love will be most clearly and mutually expressed.

2. I'm not minimizing the importance of doctrine here. I agree that we need to believe the right things about God. But that's not the basis of our fellowship, and it's not a condition for love. Jesus did not tell His friends that they would be known for their doctrine. He told them they would be known for their love.

CHAPTER 12

FOLLOWING JESUS AS LOVER AND LORD—EVEN WHEN IT'S HARD

Nothing came easily on one of my recent trips to Pakistan. We spent months planning an event and put a six-figure investment into the preparations. But our team faced resistance every step of the way.

I was beaten up in many ways during that time; I had vertigo for nine months, experienced other physical problems, and heard a voice that kept telling me, "You're not going to make it."

As the time approached to travel into the region, most flights were canceled because of conflict between India and Pakistan. There were bombings, planes were shot down, and our venue looked like it was in the middle of a war zone.

I know enough about God not to see those kinds of things as evidence of His will. If anything, this kind of resistance can be a sign of good things to come. The enemy will do anything to prevent a breakthrough.

So we continued with the process. And a lot of people thought I was crazy.

I managed to find a flight to Qatar, but we still did not have a way to get into Pakistan. Eventually a flight opened up, and we entered the country. But a storm followed us all along the way. It kept pounding the region with rain and darkness.

The hotel was damp like a dungeon. The temperature of the room seemed to suddenly drop ten degrees. Water filled up the stadium where we planned to meet and destroyed everything.

I felt like I was fighting for every single inch, every single moment of every single day in every area of life.

In that hotel room, I felt like I was about to lose it all—like I was about to die. And then we got the news that the event was canceled.

Almost a whole year of planning. More than a hundred thousand dollars raised. Gone.

But then, when I was feeling like I was at the end of my rope, God's presence came. For a moment, I felt like I was in the warmth of the Father's living room, not a damp, dark hotel room.

I had been meditating on John 20:19–23—the time when the disciples were hiding out in a room the day after the resurrection, when they were still afraid of the religious leaders, and Jesus just appeared in their midst.

I don't know how you would feel if Jesus suddenly appeared in your room, but I think you might need to hear some words of reassurance.

That's where Jesus started with His friends. He reassured them. He did several things in that encounter that changed the disciples' perspective on life.

First, He demonstrated His presence. He showed up. Maybe that seems like an obvious point, but it's really the most important part, isn't it? For the disciples, it meant they could stop wondering if He was really alive. There He was, right in front of them.

Wow! The atmosphere changed immediately.

Then Jesus imparted His peace: *"Peace be with you."*

He pointed out His provision—the wounds in His hands and side. He presented the evidence that He was still their healer, provider, wisdom, authority, power, strength, sufficiency, everything they could possibly ever need.

He gave them a purpose: "As the Father has sent Me, I also send you."

That's mission impossible. They could never go out in the same way that Jesus had come without supernatural strength. They would need His presence and power.

So He imparted His power. He breathed on them and said, *"Receive the Holy Spirit."* Just as the Spirit breathed on Adam back in Eden, the face of love breathed the power of love into the people of love. That is a beautiful snapshot of Love in the flesh imparting love to many others who would become love in the flesh—an incarnation of love as it was happening.

And He gave them a new paradigm—the forgiveness that can only be carried and released through supernatural love. He sent them out as agents of divine forgiveness.[1]

Back in that room in Pakistan, Jesus made me aware of His presence. He imparted His peace to me, just as He did with His disciples. He showed me His hands and His side—His provision. He breathed on me with His power.

He changed the atmosphere.

"Whatever you need, Leif, I am."

And my only response—the only response we can give when Jesus shows up with His presence—was "Yes, Lord. You are."

I slept for two hours. I had been thrown off the horse, but I got back on and had some room to run.

Love shows up in a time of need. I could not have gone on if He had not. I really think I might have died there that day.

I ended up in a vehicle for the next eight hours after those two hours of sleep. My back was in pain, my vertigo was still acting up, I had a migraine, the rain was still coming down, but I knew the presence of Jesus.

With my natural eyes, I could see nothing that had actually changed. But when you have an encounter with love, you can handle the process of love. Through my spiritual eyes, everything looked different.

We were heading to a wedding of two very important people. A huge tent had been set up, and the storm was threatening to tear it down. The wedding would be destroyed.

But when we drove up to the wedding site, we were surrounded by people saying, *"Allahu akbar* [God is great]. When the ambassador of love came, the rain stopped!"

I looked around, and there was a circle around the tent where no rain was falling. All around that circle, it continued to pour.

"How did you come into the country?" they asked. They couldn't believe someone would get into the war zone—or would even want to come.

"If they are going to bomb you, they will have to bomb me too," I said. "No greater love has a person than to lay down his life for his friends."

Somehow my words spread to others, and I got to speak in the mosque. I talked about love. I met with imams and generals. The meeting was put on the news for forty million people to see. It opened up favor for the whole nation.

Yes, our event had been canceled. But the Father's love is never canceled, and it always reaches someone. Sometimes it reaches whole nations.

You will see both an encounter and a process in that story because both are important parts of the journey of love. You won't experience just one or the other.

I don't ever want to give the impression that the journey of love is always easy or always pleasant. It is beautiful, rich, full, meaningful, and fulfilling. But sometimes it can be very hard.

Even in the things that are hard, Jesus is there. That's what makes this journey beautiful.

One of the darkest seasons of my life was in 2006, and it was the only time in my life I struggled with depression. My fuel tank was empty. I could not sleep. One night an angel came into my totally dark bedroom and lit it up. It stood right there in front of me, and eventually it went away. The next night a smaller angel who looked like a warrior came in. I don't normally see in the spirit realm, but I needed those moments. They didn't change everything, but they gave me a little more fuel to keep going.

My point is that you don't get to a place of cruising and being filled up all the time. That dark experience happened years after my baptism in love, and I needed another encounter to get through it. That experience in Pakistan also happened many years afterward, and I needed another breakthrough. The Father knows that. Jesus appears in the room at just the right times. The presence, peace, and provision are not given once for all time. We need them again and again.

My first encounter—my baptism of love when I lay on the floor and felt the liquid love of God flowing through me—was extreme. They had to carry me through the room. Sometimes it's not quite as dramatic as that, but it is always supernatural.

You need supernatural strength to carry supernatural glory. The glory encounters come in a moment, but the foundation that holds them comes over time. When I have experienced a supernatural encounter, I have known that it would crush me if the cracks in my foundation remained. So the process is about building up the foundation so you can carry some of the beautiful things Papa God wants to give you.

Are you pursuing encounters with Papa's love? That's very good. Keep doing that.

But don't pursue them without also paying attention to your foundation. Give God time to make it strong. Let the process play out and participate with what He is doing.

I have never doubted my Papa's love since that baptism encounter in 2000, but that doesn't mean I've walked in complete fullness ever since. I'm still in a process.

So are you.

You need encounters with God's love. You need to be over-whelmed by His heart. You also need to welcome the processes that come before, during, and after.

Like so much of life in the Kingdom of God, this is a matter of finding the rhythm.

We lean back into the Father's love and rest there. We lean forward into the world and release it. We lean back again and rest some more, then forward again and release, and on and on.

What we receive, we become. What we become, we release. What we release, we need to receive again.

Don't forget that this is a journey. And Jesus wants to walk it with you.

I love the story at the end of Luke about two followers of Jesus who were traveling the afternoon after His resurrection. He walked up beside them and asked them what they were talking about. They were somehow prevented from recogniz-ing Him, and they told Him the story of the last few days—how this prophet named Jesus was mighty in words and deeds but was handed over to the authorities and crucified. They told Him about the past and the future, but they didn't understand the past, and they didn't know what the future held. Only when He revealed Himself to them later did He begin to explain what these events meant.

That is a wonderful picture of how Jesus comes to us in the midst of crisis situations. We try to understand what happened and talk about how things are going, but we need to walk with Jesus to know where we are headed and why we are headed there.

You probably are not looking for a journey in the midst of your crises. If you are like most people, you want a quick fix. When you're hurting, you want to be healed right away. When you're facing huge mountains, you command them to move and hope they obey pretty soon.

Meanwhile, Jesus comes alongside to walk with you and lead you. He does not always want to fix things immediately. Sometimes He just wants the journey.

So Love invites us on a journey with Him. He is raising up an army of lovers, and He will not be choosing those who feel qualified or have it all together.

> *"Come to Me, all you who labor and are heavy laden, and I will give you rest," He said. "Take My yoke upon you and learn from Me, for I am gentle and lowly in heart, and you will find rest for your souls. For My yoke is easy and My burden is light"* (Matthew 11:28–30).

Do you think you're harassed, weighed down, overburdened, at the end of your rope? Great! That is the perfect place to begin. This is just the right place to receive love.

Love never tells us we have to get cleaned up in order to come. We simply need to receive and start walking where He takes us.

I love how Jesus puts it in this invitation. He does not bully people into learning how to love.

His commandment is not a military order.

He is not demanding subservience.

He is calling His friends to take His yoke, and then He assures them that His yoke is easy and the burden is light.

Most of us are not familiar with that picture, but if you came from an agricultural society, you would be. A yoke is a shaped wooden beam that fits over the necks of two animals—usually oxen or horses—so they can pull a plow or cart in unison.

And it clearly means there is some labor involved. These animals are being put to work.

But in real farm life, the yoke can be tight, and the cart or plow they are pulling can be very heavy.

That is not how it is with Jesus. His yoke binds us to Him, and it's easy on us. He does not weigh us down. And since He does the heavy lifting—99 percent of the load or more is His—we can walk along with Him in His strength.

Love in the flesh is not a bully. He is not demanding. He does not tell us to bow down and obey. He says, "Come along with Me. I am gentle and meek at heart. Learn from Me." He has the character and nature described in First Corinthians 13.

Does that mean there are no valleys or hardships along the way? Of course not. You and I both know from experience that there are. He is gentle and meek, but the road has many obstacles. His yoke is easy and His burden is light, but there is still a cross to carry.

This is where many Christians today get confused. If we receive all the blessings that Jesus stands to inherit, why are we carrying a cross? Didn't He already carry it for us?

Yes and no. He carried the cross we could never carry on our own. He paid the penalty for our sin by exchanging His life for ours. But He also called us to follow Him. And the places He went were not always easy.

Do you remember what He said to the disciples when He breathed His Spirit into them? He told them they were being sent out in the same way the Father had sent Him. (See John 20:21.)

He is Love in the flesh, sent by the Father as an incarnation of perfect love.

He sends us in just the same way—to be love in the flesh, millions of incarnations of the Father's perfect love.

In a world that rejected this kind of love when Jesus brought it, we know we are going to face opposition too.

I believe one reason this is so difficult to embrace for so many believers is that we are living in a season when the individual is king, and many Christians have borrowed that perspective from the world and talk to God as if He is there to serve them. Self is at the center.

Too many people want a resurrection without a crucifixion, a Sunday without the Friday, a new life without ever giving up the old one. Or a Lover without a Lord.

But Jesus told another story. You gain your life by losing it—by letting go of your hold on everything and surrendering it to the Father. If we are going to follow in the footsteps of Jesus, our journey will involve a cross.[2]

This is what I remind people of when they tell me they want to do what I have done and experience what I have experienced but do not realize the costly journey that has come with it. You cannot have the benefit of love without going through the school of love.

We go through training for reigning.

We are pruned in order to bear fruit.

A wilderness often comes before the promised land.

That is how God's Kingdom works.

This is why it's so important to remember that Jesus is both Lord and Lover. We are beloved, but we are also followers. He is gentle and meek, but He is also authority. His yoke is easy, but the cross we carry is not. We get a new life, but it belongs to Him.

That means freedom from the burden of a kingdom of self or a life without perfect love. But it also means we are His.

Remember the Tower of Babel? The world wants to offer success without the Holy Spirit, prosperity without presence, a kingdom without the King. Secular society pursues things that look like the Kingdom, but I think it is very clear that society does not want the King as part of the package.

Jesus never said, "I'm giving you ease." He said His *yoke*— the bond of His authority—is easy. But it is still His authority.

When we seek ease without the yoke, we are following the ways of the world. We are participating in the futility of humanity—people trying to build their own kingdom and make a name for themselves.

When you pray, "Lord, Your Kingdom come, Your will be done on earth as it is in Heaven," are you aware that you are also sometimes praying for your own will not to be done and for your kingdom not to come? You may want a quick solution, but the King is interested in the journey that leads to the solution no matter how long it takes.

"Your will be done" is a lifestyle of love because love yields to its Lord.

Near the end of Jesus's ministry, we see how perfect love was expressed through obedience to the things He suffered.

Love very often comes in the context of pain.

When Jesus's friend Lazarus died and his sisters grieved, Jesus wept with them because He loved them so much. (See John 11:35.)

When Lazarus's sister Mary realized the sacrifice Jesus would make, she lovingly and sacrificially anointed His feet with extremely costly perfume. (See John 12:1–3.)

When Peter cut the ear off of a servant of the high priest, Jesus lovingly healed him. (See John 18:10–11; Luke 22:47–51.)

When Peter denied that he ever knew Jesus, Jesus lovingly restored him. (See John 21:15–17.)

All of these situations—and many more—were demonstrations of love, but they also involved pain. Loving hearts have compassion, and compassion sometimes hurts.

One of the big questions that comes up in life and in Scripture is not whether we will experience suffering as we follow Jesus but how we respond when we do. What happens to our love?

That's where the Gospel gives us the ultimate victory. Yes, the supernatural power of God gives us miracles, healings, deliverance, and other demonstrations of power. But it also fills us with eternal love, which anchors us in eternity, which makes us invincible—more than conquerors in Christ. (See Romans 8:37.) Which is the bigger deal: the miracles or the love?

Here's a clue. God *does* miracles. God *is* love.

Miracles are something that love does. So start with love.

Jesus assured us that we would have troubles in this world. He also assured us that He had overcome that world. (See John 16:33.) Perfect Love in the flesh invited us into His fellowship, and His overcoming is our overcoming.

His journey becomes our journey.

His ministry becomes our ministry.

His love becomes our love.

And with the promise of His Spirit, we discover that the incarnation is more than just the perfect love of the divine family coming to earth in the flesh.

We become love in the flesh too.

Notes

1. It may be helpful to read this whole passage with an eye on each of these elements: the presence, peace, provision, purpose, power, and paradigm that Jesus released to His friends in John 20:19–23.

2. A theology of suffering is missing or very faint in many Christians' beliefs. I'm not referring here to a theology of sickness—I do believe God wants to heal us—but of suffering and the adversity that comes from following Jesus. The Bible is very clear on this (see John 15:18–21; 2 Tim. 3:12). The baptism of love doesn't just get rid of our pain and adversity; it comes into those places to heal and redeem.

REFLECTING ON SECTION 2

Questions to Think and Pray Through

- Jesus was first being affirmed and secure in the Father's love, then engaged in intense prayer and challenges with sickness and demonic activity, and then cried out in a crisis moment about being forsaken. In what ways do we tend to reverse this order? How have you seen this reversal at work in your own life?

- How do you think your experiences in life would change if you could live without fear? How might a fearless perspective have led you to some different decisions from those you made in the past?

- Do you agree with this statement from chapter 6: "A baptism in love is the most important requirement for success in life and ministry"? Why or why not? How does a baptism of love change the way you live? What would you do differently in life if you knew you had an A-plus on your report card before you began?

- What is the difference between living toward the Father's love and living from the Father's love? Why is it so necessary to be immersed in Heaven's love in order to represent it on earth?

- In what ways have you noticed people becoming more polarized and divided? What does love look like in these situations? Have you ever felt as if you were being pushed into categories that do not fit you very well? When people tried to put Jesus into categories, He always came up with a third option. In what ways did this enable Him to continue loving people from all sides?

Vision Exercise

Frequently and confidently envision yourself as an incarnation of love. Imagine what that looks like in each day's circumstances.

Prayer

Ask Papa God to help you be a good steward of your encounters with His love as well as the processes between those encounters. Pray for the confidence to live with His "well done" even before you do anything for Him.

Next Step

Think about a polarizing argument or controversy in our society today and try to envision a third option—a Jesus-like response that does not fit into the categories people normally create. Once you have done that, identify a way to put that response into practice, even if it is just a small step at first. Begin training yourself in this "third option" lifestyle of love.

SECTION III

OUT

Let's go back to the beginning again—to the perfect family and the love before time.

This world was created as an expression of that love because that's what love does. It reaches out, it brings in, it looks for ways to express itself.

We have seen how God expressed His love in Eden, in His people throughout history, in the incarnation of the Son, who is Love in the flesh. And we have seen how the Holy Spirit breathes that love into the beloved, the people who have accepted the invitation to receive it.

The Holy Spirit has woven—and continues to weave—the thread of love throughout God's story.

But the ultimate goal is not just a thread. This is going somewhere much bigger—an immersion, a filling, a saturation of this world into the ocean of the Father's love.

How do we know this? For one thing, this is the direction of Scripture from its beginning to its very end. But there are also clear statements in Scripture of God's ultimate purpose.

One of them is in the short prophecy of Habakkuk: *"The earth will be filled with the knowledge of the glory of the Lord, as the waters cover the sea"* (Habakkuk 2:14). If you are observant, you might have noticed that this verse does not say anything about love. At least not on the surface.

To see love in it, we need to take a look at this idea of glory. Remember, John's Gospel begins by talking about the Word in the flesh, who is also Love in the flesh. And as John writes, *"We beheld His glory...full of grace and truth"* (John 1:14)

In the very next chapter, John points out that Jesus's first miracle, which was an act of love at a wedding feast, was an example of Jesus manifesting His glory. (See John 2:11.)

The hosts had run out of wine. That would have been very embarrassing for them, and it might have ended the celebration early, or at least made it much less of a celebration. So Jesus, persuaded by His mother and without calling any attention to Himself, turned many gallons of water into wine. He saved the day for the hosts. We might think that this miracle would have brought more glory to Him if more people had known, but not very many people did. The only people who knew were the servants who poured the wine, Jesus's mother, and some of the disciples. It was very quiet for a miracle.

Yet according to John, this was the first occasion of Jesus manifesting His glory. Why did John think this was glorious? Not because it was a demonstration of power. The demonstration was seen by only a few people. It was glorious because it was an act of love that affected many.

Way back in the days of Moses, at a time when God's relationship with His people seemed to be in question (at least from Moses's point of view), this great prophet asked God to show him His glory. God said yes to that request but told Moses he would not be allowed to see God's face.

So with Moses standing in the cleft of a rock to hide him from the fullness of God's presence, which would have been overwhelming and even devastating for a mortal human being, God passed by. And His words to Moses as He passed are very revealing: *"The Lord, the Lord, the compassionate and gracious God, slow to anger, abounding in love and faithfulness, maintaining love to thousands, and forgiving wickedness, rebellion and sin."*[1]

The literal sense of the phrase *"love to thousands"* is not thousands of *people* but thousands of *generations*. In other words, throughout all of history. Love from before time would extend through the human story from beginning to end—like a thread woven throughout time.

Do you see the connection? Moses asked to see God's glory. God said, "Okay, here is My faithful love." That is the glory, or at least a huge part of it. The glory of God is His nature, and His nature is love.

As John so clearly wrote later, *"God is love"* (1 John 4:8, 16). He *has* glory, but love is who He is. So if He expresses His nature, and that expression is a manifestation of glory, then His glory is very much a display of His love.

When Habakkuk writes that God's glory is going to cover the earth, we can assume that God's love will cover the earth because His glory is characterized by His love.

Jesus makes that connection too. When He was praying the night before His crucifixion, He talked to the Father about love and glory. And He was very insistent on sharing both with those who follow Him. *"The glory which You gave Me I have given them,"* He said (John 17:22). And then He prayed that the world would know that the Father loved them as Jesus loved them (see John 17:23) and that the love that God had put into Jesus would also be put into them—as Jesus Himself was being put into them. (See John 17:26.)

Glory, love, the presence of God, and unity with Him are woven throughout this prayer as variations on the same theme. In this prayer, glory is an aspect of love, and love is an aspect of glory.

I love how Paul captured this when he prayed for the heart of the Gospel to go deep into his readers' hearts:

> *That He would grant you, according to the riches of His glory, to be strengthened with might through His Spirit in the inner man, that Christ may dwell in your hearts through faith; that you, being rooted and grounded in love, may be able to comprehend with all the saints what is the width and length and depth and height—to know the love of Christ which passes knowledge; that you may be filled with all the fullness of God* (Ephesians 3:16–19).

Notice again that there is a connection here between glory and love. This is a prayer for Christians to be supernaturally filled with Christ Himself and with His love—and to be given supernatural strength to comprehend it. How? According to God's riches in glory.

So God's glory/love is going to cover the earth like the waters cover the sea—which means deeply and everywhere, since waters *are* the sea—and filling the earth with His glory means filling His people with love.

You should be seeing a very strong connection in this with our purpose. How is God's glory going to cover the earth? Through His people. To be a little more specific, through His people who love like He does. He is baptizing His beloved who are made in His image and restored to His image so we will take His glory/love into all the earth.

This is our mission. We are agents of glory and love who are sent out to fill the earth with glory and love. And we are called to do it so thoroughly that the world is absolutely, completely, inseparably covered with love.

Total saturation.

But total saturation does not begin with saturation. It begins with a trickle, then a flow, then an immersion, or as I said earlier, a seed, then a tree, and then a forest.

It begins with an awareness, then an encounter and a process (or many encounters and processes), then a lifestyle of convergence in which we align our hearts with the heart of the Father.

We receive love, give love, become love, and release love—all over the earth.

If you ever felt like you needed a higher calling or a mission to keep you going, this is it. This is how God calls out the real you into an authentic journey, and along the way in that journey you begin to feel like you're alive in new ways.

That journey, as we've seen, will involve dramatic encounters with the Spirit of God, who breathes out the love of God into human beings, and it will involve seemingly ordinary processes—also with the Spirit of God, breathing in His love moment by moment. But it's all divine, all supernatural, and all good.

And somewhere in that journey, you will begin to love yourself as the Father loves you. You will start to see yourself as the Father sees you. And because you have received perfect, supernatural love, you begin to love others as the Father has loved you. And then you help others love themselves and others with the same kind of love because they too have received that perfect, supernatural love from the Father.

You will find that this kind of love encounter—which is much, *much* more than just an encounter—is the power that changes environments. It breaks strongholds, melts fear, heals souls and bodies, and transforms cultures.

It keeps going and going.

Until the glory of God covers the earth like the waters cover the sea.

Note

1. Exodus 34:6–7 (NIV). Granted, this is not the entire declaration, and God did go on to say that He punished sin to the third and fourth generation. But three and four generations pale in comparison to the thousands of generations to whom He promised His love.

CHAPTER 13

SENT-OUT SONS AND DAUGHTERS

A young man in Norway got a glimpse of God's heavenly glory in 1796, and it changed him forever. He looked back on it later as the most important turning point in his life. He was suddenly filled with and overpowered by the presence of God. The experience gave him "a powerful love of him and my neighbour."[1]

This was a baptism in the Spirit. And the way he described it, it was also a baptism in love. But this was not just a beautiful experience. This baptism led to something significant. It changed many lives, the culture, and the history of a nation.

Hans Nielsen Hauge suddenly saw the world differently. He saw the brokenness of the people around him—how they were limited by the elitist teachings and culture of the dominant church. Within a few months, he was crossing the country on foot and on skis to teach people and pray for them to receive the same kind of encounter he had received.

He was just one person—a marginalized outsider in Norway's religious culture—who realized the power of love to give wisdom, power, courage, faith, and innovative ideas to ordinary people just like him.

Hauge encountered a lot of opposition from the established church and the Denmark-Norway government (they were united at the time). It was illegal for laypeople like him to preach or hold unsupervised meetings, but he and his followers traveled constantly throughout the country to preach in small gatherings.

He spent a lot of time in prison, but the government got him out when they needed his help because they realized he had access to answers to problems they could not solve. He and the peasant workers he influenced knew how to start businesses, transform economies and systems, and bless society in a multitude of ways.

Even though he didn't have much education, Hauge wrote books that reached hundreds of thousands of people. He loosened the grip of rigid religion on the spiritual climate of his nation. And because many of his followers emigrated to America, his influence was international and continued for generations across continents.

I had the honor of visiting the farm where Hauge grew up. I have followed in his footsteps where he traveled the country, and I've seen the jail in Fredrikstad where he was imprisoned. He paid a terrible price for the love he gave to his nation. But the by-product of that love was being able to have courage, overcome many challenges, forgive those who hurt him, and live and love in such a way that he raised up a generation of nation changers. Even the constitution of Norway was influenced by many of his followers. Hauge is one of the reasons Norway went from being one of the poorest nations in Europe to one of the richest in the world.

Once when Loren Cunningham, the founder of YWAM, was visiting King Harald of Norway, he pointed out the country's wonderful education system and all the benefits and freedoms the people enjoyed, in contrast to the kingdom's conditions just a few generations ago. "How do you explain such a rapid change?" he asked.

"I am asked that question by ambassadors all the time," King Harald answered. "And I do not know how to explain it."

"Would you like to hear about the person who changed your country, your majesty?" Cunningham asked. And he began to tell the story of Hans Nielsen Hauge and the love that motivated him.[2]

One person can have such an encounter with power and love that it changes him from ordinary to extraordinary. But it does not change him alone. The Father's love that had touched Hauge transformed the world around him.

That is always one of the purposes of God's transforming love.

We receive it in personal, intimate moments with the Father, then the Son sends us out, and then the Holy Spirit magnifies it in our lives. It becomes a catalyst for something bigger.

Did you get that? The fruit of your private moments do not remain private. They may even change history. It is very important to steward them well.

Love Flows in, Love Flows Out

Have you ever gone swimming in a river? If so, you've stood at the edge and taken a first step in. Immediately, you are ankle-deep. Wade a little bit farther, and you're up to your knees. Keep going, and the water is waist-level. Then chest-level. Then up to your neck. And if you really want to go for it, you let yourself go all the way under.

Intimacy with God is much like that. You can go in ankle-deep. You can keep going and let the water flow past your knees, your waist, your neck, or even over your head. You can keep pressing in for a day, a season, or a lifetime. But many people don't go that far. They stop when they've had just a bit, a trickle, a little affirmation that yes, God is there, you and He are connecting, and all is well until the next time.

God gave Ezekiel a prophetic picture of this kind of river. The prophet was shown waters coming out of the temple in Jerusalem that gave life everywhere they flowed. At first, the river was just ankle-deep, then it was knee-deep, then waist-deep, and then it as too deep to cross.

This is how the Father's love and the Holy Spirit's power works in our lives. This vision has several meanings at different levels, but one of them is to represent our experience of the presence of God. And if this river represents God's presence, it must also represent the flow of love into our hearts.

Some people think they are satisfied with a taste of it. Others cannot be satisfied with just a taste. They know they need more. Some keep on going because they can never get enough. They want total immersion, a baptism in an ocean of love in the depths of their spirit. But they also want more than a baptism. They want an ongoing flow.

God has enough love for that. You can swim in that ocean of love. There's enough for you to go to the nations and represent His heart to multitudes.

I encourage you to dream big like that, but also to go ahead and start representing love where you are. You can envision huge revivals and movements sweeping across nations and regions and the world, but there also has to be enough love in you for your wife or husband, your children, your boss, and your neighbor.

Many people long for the kind of love that transforms nations but have trouble with the kind of love that reaches out to a difficult relative or neighbor. They want the Father's love for ministry purposes but do not pursue it for family or community purposes. All of it is available, but it does not work well just to go for helpings of certain kinds of love like they are items on a buffet. If you want to go for it all, then it is very important to go for it *all*.

But you will also need to recognize seasons in your life. Revelations of love come in waves, with God preparing you for the times that are coming and then giving you more when you are entering into a new season. And at least some of His reasons for doing that are up to you. You often get from Him whatever you are prepared to give to others.

Remember God's purpose from the very beginning—to fill the earth with His people who bear His image. To put this another way, to fill the earth with His glory through the people who will carry it.

This is why the heavenly family of love created human beings, why the Son of love became Love in the flesh, and why He breathed the Holy Spirit into His followers.

You were made for this mission, but you cannot carry it out unless you meet God in a place of intimacy and let Him love you. This intimacy may begin with droplets and trickles of His presence and love, but an increase is always available to those who steward these foretastes.

The Journey from a Foretaste of Love to an Inheritance of Love

I love the story of how Jacob became Israel because there are lessons of both identity and intimacy in it. But it especially teaches us about inheritance.

We saw how Jacob was a wrestler—figuratively in his maneuverings against his brother and literally in an encounter with God. He obtained his brother's birthright and blessing, and he had to flee to escape his brother's wrath.

But God saw Jacob through the lenses of his destiny, not his history. He gave him an open-Heaven encounter and restated the promises He had once given Abraham and applied them to Jacob's descendants. But for Jacob, this was a foretaste of love. His heart could not yet receive more than a visitation.

That would happen later when he surrendered to God and received a new name, then got up with love and humility in his heart. He had spent his life fighting for blessings, and then he ended up wrestling for one. At the moment he was most vulnerable, he held on and insisted on receiving a blessing. And God gave it to him.

Up to that point, Jacob had done the best a man can do in working for God. After that moment, God would show Jacob what He can do through a man.

That's what a new identity does for someone. It changes things. It makes everyone look different because we are now seeing through the eyes of love. It also sets us up for our inheritance.

Jacob's new name, Israel, refers to someone who strives with God or is triumphant with God. But it can also mean "prince," which points to a royal inheritance that we cannot get as long as we have orphan hearts. God does not trust just anyone with His inheritance. He gives it to those who know who they are and who walk in His love.

The inheritance of Abraham and Isaac began to flow through Jacob. The twelve tribes that came from his children formed a nation also called Israel.

When the writer of Hebrews wrote about Jacob, he mentioned three things: Jacob blessed the sons of Joseph, his grandchildren, before he died; he worshipped; and he leaned on his staff. (See Hebrews 11:21.)

That is a very odd combination of facts to remember. What is the point of this verse in Hebrews? I think blessing Joseph's two sons, even when he was old and nearly blind, means he could still see in the spirit. With echoes of his own experience years before, he crossed his arms and blessed the younger before the older. He was not stuck in the natural order of things; he saw into the supernatural.

The importance of his worship is very clear. But the fact that Jacob built altars and worshipped wherever he went is what sons and daughters of inheritance do. Many people worship God in order to get a blessing, but children of inheritance worship because they love God.

And then leaning on his staff represents rest. Jacob had learned how to rest in the Father's house. He knew who he was and was no longer striving to become someone. His posture reflected a man who is finally at peace.

These are vital aspects of transformation for sent-out sons and daughters to cling to. When we get our new identity and new name, when we begin to see through the lens of love, when our orphan hearts have been adopted into the heavenly family and filled with the Father's love we

- no longer strive but live from a place of rest;
- see God, ourselves, and others differently—as if we are looking into the face of God;
- begin walking in our inheritance;
- see miracles of reconciliation and restoration;
- see into the supernatural realm and live under an open Heaven; and
- never forget that we are beloved sons and daughters of God in whom He is well pleased.

Are you a Jacob or an Israel? Are you still striving to become or have you gotten to that place of surrender, where God gives you a new name and fills your heart with His love?

When you go into a hostile world, can you see the face of God like Jacob saw when he looked at Esau? Have you begun looking at others by their potential rather than their past?

When the world looks at you, do they see someone at rest in the Father's love? Do they see a worshipper? Do they recognize in you a demonstration of supernatural love and honor and a source of supernatural blessing?

If you have been able to look into the face of God through your intimacy with Him—if you have become saturated with His love—many things are going to change in your life.

Some who sought to harm you will embrace you instead.

Your rest in Him will position you to receive from Him and reign with Him.

The Spirit in you will change the environment around you.

The open Heaven above you will bring signs and wonders to you and through you.

You will steward your inheritance, increase it, and bless with it.

You will not just be "sent out." You will be sent out in the manner of Jesus, on the mission of Jesus, and with the manifestations of Jesus.

You will become and release the love you have received.

Notes

1. As quoted in Alv Johan Magnus, "Revival and Society: An Examination of the Haugian Revival and Its Influence on Norwegian Society in the 19th Century" (master's thesis, University of Oslo, 1978). Magnus got the original quote from Hans Nielsen Hauge's letters as published in Brev frå Hans Nielsen Hauge by Ved Ingolf Kvamen.

2. Loren Cunningham with Janice Rogers, *The Book That Transforms Nations: The Power of the Bible to Change Any Country* (Seattle, WA: YWAM Publishing, 2007), 66.

CHAPTER 14

BECOMING LOVE AMBASSADORS

A Samaritan woman once encountered Love in the flesh at a well in her hometown.[1] This very unlikely recipient of love came to a very unlikely place to have a life-changing experience.

But this woman desperately needed that kind of encounter. Samaritans were not loved by most Jews. In fact, many Jews hated them. Samaritans had been told that they were outside of God's covenant. This Samaritan woman did not have a great reputation; men had their way with her and then left her to take care of herself. She came to the well at a very odd time, in the middle of the day, perhaps to avoid the stares of other women in the village.

Yet Love in the flesh talked to her—a woman, a sinner, a Samaritan—with openness and acceptance. She was not used to that.

It took some time for love to break through. But when it did, this woman's life changed.

She had to learn who she was—her true identity.

She had to look past the barriers of religion and tradition to see a relationship and a new way of life.

She had to grasp that a new season was upon her.

She had to leave behind her water jar—her means of survival—and step into life beyond just surviving.

She needed to be set free. And when she came face to face with love, she found freedom.

The way the story is often told, that is the end of it. An unloved woman experienced love and was set free. But this is not where the story ends in Scripture. Not only was this woman's life changed, her village was changed through her testimony.

The outcast received love, and then the Samaritans in her town received love because she could not keep it to herself. In fact, this wounded woman, now healed, went to the very people who had wounded her—the men of the village—and showed them the way of healing too.

Glory covered a Samaritan community, which is a wonderful start to covering the earth.

This Samaritan woman actually became a forerunner of revival.[2] She was a carrier of the kind of truth and love that transforms, not because she was well qualified or had been trained but because she received the love of Jesus and took up His yoke. Her brokenness qualified her to receive love, and love qualified her to minister in love to her village.

And Jesus used that remarkable occasion to teach His disciples about the coming harvest. He actually stayed in this village for two days to show love to these hated Samaritans and give His friends a case study in how these things work.

Before that, when the disciples first returned from their errand and discovered the commotion Jesus had caused, He cast a vision for them. He talked about the season of harvest—how people can look at the fields and figure out that three or four months are left before harvest time. But the spiritual harvest of love—the seeds that had grown into trees that were ready to bear fruit—was already right there in front of them. Others had planted and labored, and now it was time to reap. To connect this invitation into the harvest to God's plan to cover the earth with His glory, people were ready for demonstrations of supernatural love.

And they still are.

You Are a Carrier of Authentic, Supernatural Love

In fact, people who are not well acquainted with supernatural love may be more ready than they have ever been for demonstrations of it.

They are not hungry for our doctrine.

They are not convinced by our debates.

They are not flocking to our conferences.

But they are moved by our love when we carry it authentically within us. This is not just love, but *supernatural* love, the perfect love of the divine family from before time—unconditional, unchanging, undeniable, timeless.

This is the kind of love Love in the flesh breathed into His followers when He told them to receive the Holy Spirit so they could become love in the flesh too.

Do you remember when we talked about the fact that some laws are higher than others? Jesus pointed out two commandments as being above all the rest: loving God and loving neighbors.

Far too many Christians are out there trying to convince the world of the truth of the Gospel through their arguments, their politics, and their theology. Some seem to think that changing laws is the same as changing hearts.

Please do not misunderstand me here. It is very important to be engaged in the "culture wars" and government. We are called to influence every area of society, to season our culture, and shine our light on it everywhere we go.

If you are not familiar with the seven-mountain paradigm, this is its primary message. The seven "mountains" of society are government, media, economy, arts and entertainment, education, family, and religion. These are our spheres of influence, and it is vital for believers to be fully engaged in the ones they are called to be involved with.

We do not go into each "mountain" to enforce our morality but to influence with our kindness.

Past generations of Christians have not always done this. Many people abandoned the entertainment industry, the media, the economic arena, public schools, the messy business of politics, and then started talking about how these were all under the influence of the world.

Of course they were under the influence of the world. Christians left them and stopped having influence there.

I think we've learned by now that our calling is not to escape society or isolate from it. We are called to go into it, to be salt and light wherever we are, to carry the influence of the Kingdom into all the dark and lonely places by the way we love.

This is how the world is changed.

But it has to happen in the right spirit. If we go into the seven mountains of society without love, our efforts are worthless, as Paul said. (See First Corinthians 13:1–3.)

John was just as clear: *"Everyone who loves is born of God and knows God. He who does not love does not know God, for God is love"* (1 John 4:7–8).

It is counterproductive for us to contend for the Kingdom of God without carrying the nature of God. And the nature of God is love.

Think about the areas of society you are involved in. Have you ever wondered, *What would supernatural love look like here?*

What would it look like in schools? In government? In media? In business? In arts and entertainment?

We can even ask what it would look like in churches, since sometimes what we see in churches is not supernatural love.

How do we give honor in each of these places? How do we let love shape the culture in each one? How can we be catalysts for movements of love that sweep over an organization or institution, a community, or a city?

Are we waiting for God to demonstrate love apart from us? That is not how He does things. He is moving His people into every arena of society's institutions and activities for us to represent Him in all those places, even the darkest ones.

This is how people see God—through our love. Jesus was very clear about this. (See John 13:35.) Signs and wonders do much more to convince them of His goodness than arguments do, but even signs and wonders have to be motivated by love. Love is the environment that makes them possible.

If you ever need to be convinced of the transforming power of love, try it out yourself. The more you give, the more you receive.

Jesus actually told His disciples this very plainly. *"Give, and it will be given to you....For with the measure you use, it will be measured to you"* (Luke 6:38 NIV).

He was not talking there about money (though His words do apply to financial generosity). He was talking about things like kindness and forgiveness and grace—in other words, love.

So if you've ever thought, *Wow, I really need some more love,* try an experiment. Give away whatever love you have. Jesus promises that this will cause love to come pouring into your life.

In addition to your own experience, though, there are some other places you can turn to see the transforming power of love. Just read the Gospels, where Jesus transforms people's lives with love all the time.

For example, look at the story of Zacchaeus. This tax collector—that title was usually understood to be for someone who had probably abused his responsibilities in order to fill his own pockets—had heard about Jesus, saw the commotion as Jesus was approaching Jericho, and wanted a good look at Him.

Apparently, Zacchaeus was a little height challenged, so he climbed a tree for a better look. And that's when Jesus singled him out: *"Zacchaeus, come down immediately. I must stay at your house today"* (Luke 19:5 NIV).

This was not only astonishing to the crowds, who were very disturbed that Jesus would want to hang out with a cheater. It was also astonishing to Zacchaeus. This may have been the first time someone in Jericho had actually shown him some love.

Jesus could have reprimanded him, but the Bible does not tell us that He did.

If He wanted to, Jesus could have made this visit to Zacchaeus's house conditional on his willingness to give back some of the money he had extorted.

But Jesus just loved Zacchaeus. He honored him with His presence.

And did you notice how Zacchaeus responded? He repented almost immediately and promised to restore everything he had cheated out of people—four times over. And he pledged half of his possessions to the poor. (See Luke 19:8.)

That's a lot of fruit for a little bit of fellowship.

It kind of makes you wonder how the world might respond if we just loved them instead of reprimanded them.

Stories like that of the Samaritan woman and Zacchaeus demonstrate the amazing transformational power of love, but they also demonstrate that God is calling His people into His harvest. The fields are ready. He is raising up love ambassadors who will go into these fields and prioritize love over doctrine, defensiveness, and battle lines.

He is looking for carriers of authentic, supernatural love.

He is looking for people who will step into the river and keep on going until they're swimming in an ocean.

He is looking for love ambassadors who are able and willing to

- see a generous giver in the miserly Zacchaeuses of the world;
- see a Paul in the unlikely Sauls of this world;
- see a David in the very unlikely shepherds of this world;
- recognize a neighbor behind the hardened and jaded hearts of this world;
- shine light into the darkest places of this world; and
- love the people right next them—spouses, children, parents, coworkers, and neighbors.

In other words, He is seeking those who will receive His baptism of love and not let the journey end there. He searches for those who will become love and then release love wherever they go.

Walk in the Authority of Love

I heard a story years ago about a city council meeting in Pennsylvania with a very hot item on the agenda: a shelter for people with mental issues and addiction problems. Neighbors opposed the shelter, of course. Not many people want bipolar, schizophrenic addicts in the neighborhood. It looked like the shelter was going to be voted down.

A small woman walked to the front of the room, got on her knees, and pleaded for the poor and hurting. "Please receive them," she said.

The atmosphere in the room changed and people's hearts softened. This ambassador of love—Mother Teresa—who happened to be in town at the time of this meeting, knew how to walk in the authority of love.

Mother Teresa understood how to speak very directly to people in powerful positions. She had interacted with presidents, prime ministers, and kings. But that is not where her authority came from. She walked in a higher authority because she knew how to love.

This is a very important truth.

You only have authority over what you love. Many people are trying to live out a ministry of power, exorcising demons and healing the sick, without loving the people they are ministering to. That is powerless.[3]

But when you love…well, that is another story. You carry the nature of God. You cannot help but walk in authority when you love.

Perhaps this is why when Jesus delivered a message to the church at Ephesus, He encouraged them to return to their first love. He commended them for their doctrine, but that was not where their power came from. In order to do the works they had once done, they needed to go back to the love they had first experienced. They needed to return to their foundation of Papa God's perfect, supernatural love. (See Revelation 2:1–7.)

Believers in Jesus who know how to love have been given authority to represent Heaven on earth. We have received the perfect love before time and carry that atmosphere within us. We can go into difficult situations and change the environment because we are different kind of people.

Ambassadors of love think differently.

We relate to people differently.

We move in the Spirit of the Father's heart and the Son, who is Love in the flesh—and in the opposite spirit from the thief who came to steal, kill, and destroy. (See John 10:10.)

We represent abundant life and abundant love.

I woke up in Pakistan one morning to the news that a suicide bomb had killed or injured more than sixty people at a church. The thief who comes to steal, kill, and destroy is still busy, and his work cast a shadow of fear and chaos over that region.

But ambassadors of love can thrive in the midst of fear and chaos because we bring good news. Darkness actually presents an opportunity for light. We speak the language of love and honor the way Jesus honors. We bring the love of the perfect family into broken relationships and cultures. We bring the environment of Heaven into places that look and feel like hell.

Our ministry had some ambassadors of love in that region who were able to bring reconciliation. We met with Muslim and Christian leaders to help the families who suffered losses. Testimonies of Jesus began to spread, and healing began.

The same kind of healing happened the first time I went to Cambodia. I had responded to an invitation to go because I felt strongly in my spirit that I was to represent Heaven on earth there.

Darkness from the time of the killing fields was still at work in that country. The genocide stripped the country of its true identity. But wherever ambassadors of love go, we bring light and love. We represent the opposite of what we see in dark and hateful places. The thief cannot overcome that.

While I was in Cambodia, I met some members of the Khmer Rouge who had participated in those horrific crimes in the 1970s. How do you represent love in that situation? It is not easy. They had done unspeakable things.

But an encounter with Papa God's love transforms hardened hearts. And if we have learned how to see through His eyes, we see and think differently.

Love does not see people the way they are. It sees them the way they are going to be. It focuses on destiny, not history. Love looks past the natural and sees the supernatural.

So I put my arms around some of those Khmer Rouge leaders and let the Father's love show through.

I knew this was not my love. I did not have this kind of love for them. I needed to remember what I had received. But when I put my arms around them, I could sense the brokenness, the wounds, and the deception.

Broken people break things.

Healed people heal things.

I had been healed. So when I put my arms around them and started to sense the Father's love, I knew that love could heal them.

A lady came up to me that night after a service. She had never learned to read or write because the Khmer Rouge were killing all the educated people when she was young. But she wanted to be able to read the Bible.

This is not a typical prayer request in my experience. People usually come up to me to receive a baptism of love or a healing. But this woman just wanted to read.

Maybe you are wondering, *Is that part of the Gospel*" If the Son of Man came *"to seek and save that which was lost,"* it is

(Luke 19:10). Most people read their salvation theology into that verse—that Jesus came to save lost people. That is very true, but the promise is even bigger. This is about the Kingdom of God, not spiritual salvation only. Jesus came to seek and to save whatever was lost, and this woman had lost the opportunity to be literate. She could not read the Bible.

You are welcome to take that promise and apply it to other areas of your life. You have experienced losses. Everyone has. If the restoration of your losses fits into the Kingdom of God, Jesus came for that. Take Him up on it, and believe for Him to do something to restore you.

Jesus came to bring beauty out of ashes, to give joy in the place of mourning, to give us a garment of praise instead of a spirit of heaviness. Why? So we might be called trees of righteousness, as Isaiah says—a planting that demonstrates *His glory* (see Isaiah 61:3) or as we have already seen, His love.

Seeds of love grow into trees of love and become forests of love.

Khmer is a very difficult language. But when this woman opened up her Bible, tears filled her eyes. She began to read. It all made sense. She read verse after verse.

Other women who had come up for the same reason picked up the language too. Their comprehension opened up. Supernaturally, they could all read.

It was amazing. We saw Jesus restore what was lost in these women's lives. This was a manifestation of His glory and an act of His love.

What would it look like to overflow with supernatural love in your home, your workplace, your school, and your community?

If the Holy Spirit can fill us with the love of the perfect family among the nations, He can fill us with that love among relatives and neighbors. Our homes and offices can become Kingdom outposts. Heaven can touch earth.

As followers of Love in the flesh, we can become love in the flesh ourselves. The love before time can invade our times.

And yes, the Holy Spirit can take His ambassadors even to the ends of the earth, the darkest places, the most broken and hurting places, and change the environment with love.

Whether you realize it or not—and I hope that you do by now—you are an ambassador of love. You wake up in the morning with a day full of possibilities ahead of you. Everywhere you turn, there is an opportunity to show love.

If you have a family, you have the opportunity to show supernatural love to each member.

If you are in a school, you can represent the Father's warm and welcoming home there.

If you are in the media, you can communicate hope and love even in the most painful stories to tell.

If you are in business or government, you can lead and serve with the environment of Heaven within you.

Whatever you do and wherever you are, you can shift the atmosphere to feel more like the Father's living room.

All of this and more is possible because ambassadors are not waiting just for the big opportunities to love. They see opportunities *everywhere*.

Notes

1. You can read the original story in John 4:1–42.

2. Later on in the Book of Acts, Philip and then Peter and John went to preach in Samaria and found very receptive audiences, many of whom believed in Jesus and were healed and delivered (see Acts 8:4–25). Much of the fruit that occurred during that time of ministry might well have come from the breakthrough of this Samaritan woman's faith and the time Jesus spent in her town.

3. If you've ever tried to experience the power of God above the love of God, you've probably found this to be true. You cannot separate power from love in God's Kingdom, and love comes first.

CHAPTER 15

FEAR–THE ENEMY OF LOVE

Do you remember the story of Ahmad the suicide bomber? He accomplished every part of his mission except one: he did not die.

He hurt many other people, but he woke up in a military hospital and was very surprised to learn that the Americans treating him were not going to torture and humiliate him like he had always been taught. He experienced genuine kindness, maybe for the first time in his life.

Ahmad is an encouraging example of someone who seems on the surface to be unreachable. To natural human eyes, someone like that is hardened and very unlikely to change. But in Papa God's eyes, this kind of person is a prime candidate to be transformed by supernatural love.

Through your natural eyes, you may have looked at some people on the news or in your circle of acquaintances as "unreachable"—as very difficult cases that make hope seem unrealistic. In your theology, you probably know God can change any life. But these lives? Many of them look too far gone.

A woman came up to me after a conference session recently to tell me her story. She had been abused from the age of one onward. When she was twelve, she was trafficked by a satanic cult and horrifically abused over the next few years. She had lost eleven babies, some of them used as human sacrifices by the people exploiting her. She had struggled with mental illness, been on many medications, and gone through years of therapy.

As I listened to her story, I began to feel totally wrecked by the mental, physical, emotional, and spiritual torment she had experienced. I could not imagine going through everything she had suffered. It was just horrible.

I am not sure how she came to be at our meeting, but I remember that when I was preaching that day, I suddenly stopped in the middle of my message and told a story about how God had taken me back to a time when I was twelve years old and healed some deep childhood wounds with His love. I felt a little like I had done some rabbit chasing—that I'd gotten off track and interrupted my own message with a story that did not quite fit— but when this woman heard that story, she thought, *Maybe love can take me back too. Maybe there was a time in my life before pain.* She was probably in her forties now and had been tormented as long as she could remember. *But maybe,* she thought, *God could take her back to a time before the darkness.*

Suddenly, this woman felt as if she was being taken out of her own body. God took her back to a time as a little baby before the pain and began ministering to her there. She saw how He had seen her, accepted her, and adored her before she was in her mother's womb. She saw who she was intended to be in His eyes. He began healing those deep, deep wounds.

As she was telling me this story, I could see her face change at this moment. I could see her countenance shift from darkness to light. Tears began to flow. She was glowing as she described how God had touched her.

"I knew I was changed," she said. She hugged me and told me it was the first time in her life she had experienced love, felt valued, and had hope. Love had set her completely free.

At many points in her life, people could have looked at this precious woman and thought her situation was too difficult, she was too far gone, one of those hard cases, unreachable.

But God's love reached her. There are no hard cases for God. Love heals, restores, and makes all things new.

People we normally see as difficult cases are usually extremely broken hearts looking for wholeness. It does not matter if those hearts are inside a wounded and abused exterior, a terrorist, a crime boss, a homeless person on the side of the road, or a very religious Pharisee.

Everybody is searching for love. The hard cases often run from love or resist it because they have spent long years, even a lifetime, looking at evidence that authentic, supernatural love does not exist.

But their hearts know it does. Their hearts may be bound in extreme pain or bitterness, but they still know.

And one touch—or sometimes many repeated touches—from an ambassador of love carrying the authority of Heaven can break down walls, melt bitterness, and transform a life.

But an ambassador of love first needs to encounter that powerful love personally. And then we need to overcome any fear that stands in the way of expressing it.

When Fear Comes In

I often tell a story of my fear of dogs. It began when I was a small boy in Norway when a tiny dog with a very big growl bit my hand. That is when my fear entered in.

Over the years, I noticed that fear would rise up in me every time I saw a dog. I knew it. Dogs sensed it. And that fear made me avoid every situation where I thought I might encounter a dog, even when I was in no real danger at all. This lasted long into my adult life.

One day, a pit bull covered in scars from many dogfights came into my family's backyard. I had already had my baptism of love and traveled all over the world talking about it. I told people that perfect love casts out all fear. But I was still a little afraid of dogs, and this pit bull sensed it.

So there we were in the same yard. I knew I was afraid of this dog. The dog knew I was afraid of him. But neither of us knew I was about to have a breakthrough in understanding.

A thought suddenly came to me. *If our sweet little kitten was in the yard that day and this pit bull came in to attack it, would I have risked my life to save it?* I do not think so. I may be an ambassador of love, and I love kittens, but my fear would have been greater than my love in that situation.

But if my daughter had been in the yard when that pit bull came in to attack her, I would have overcome my fear in a hurry. In fact, I would not have given it a second thought. My love in that situation would have been far greater than my fear.

Do you see what is happening here? Whichever attitude or emotion is stronger in you is the one you will follow.

If you're like most people, you probably wear at least two antennae—one that recognizes opportunities to love and the other that recognizes potential rejection. These antennae send very conflicting messages to our brains, and we often feel the tension between them. "Should I show love to my unfair boss? To that neighbor who snaps at me? To that reclusive person who has shut herself off from everyone else? To that gang member with the cold stare and the battle scars?" Very often, our fear is bigger than our love.

Please do not misunderstand. Sometimes there is wisdom in being cautious. I am not advocating foolishness or recklessness. But sometimes the problem is just fear.

Whenever you find yourself thinking of opportunities to love but rejecting them because of the response you might get, your fear is bigger than your love in that situation. Fear is an enemy of love, and it often gets in the way. It steals love.

This plays out in many different ways. Fear scares us away from evangelism, praying boldly in faith for "hopeless" cases, being vulnerable with the people close to us, and going into dark places with the light of love.

If this is a problem for you, please do not worry. You are a normal human being with normal fears. But in our journey to move from being normal humans carrying remnants of the fall to supernatural humans carrying the love of the Father, this is a problem we will need to overcome. We want to enter into a higher realm of living. To put it another way, we want to live from the Father's living room, carrying that environment of perfect love with us everywhere we go.

You can begin to overcome fear by taking baby steps. Are you having trouble loving a terrorist you've seen on the news? Then start with an acquaintance who has some annoying habits or a homeless person in your neighborhood or city. Do you have little compassion for atheists, Muslims, and others who criticize Christianity? Then start with loving a Christian whose perspective is completely different from yours.

But it is important at least to start. Then you can take slightly bigger steps, then even bigger ones.

You were made to carry the love of your Father. This is how you were designed. You bear His image. Sooner or later, you will find that love fits.

Love in the Valley of Bones

Ezekiel lived among the Jewish exiles in Babylon. In a vision, God took him to a valley of dry bones. In other words, he was standing among very dead people—a place where revival looked impossible. A hopeless situation.

But God breathed hope into this situation by telling Ezekiel to prophesy life. That is what he did, and the bones began to move. Broken bones rejoined. Flesh grew. Dry bones turned into whole bodies.

But these bodies were still dead. So God told the prophet to prophesy again. He did, and God breathed life into these bodies, and they stood up—an *exceedingly great army* (Ezekiel 37:1–10). A generation of the dead came fully alive, ready to return to Israel.

This prophetic picture prepared captive Jews to hope and believe for a return to their homeland. It was given to Ezekiel at a low point in Hebrew history, when God's very own chosen people were taken into exile and their holy city was destroyed. In His tender and compassionate love, Papa God wanted them to know that a time of restoration would come.

This prophecy demonstrates that the Babylonian captivity was not a hopeless situation. But the prophecy does even more than that. It also demonstrates that no situation anywhere is hopeless.

No generation is beyond revival.

No darkness is immune to light.

No degree of death can overcome real life.

In your mission as an ambassador of love, you will find yourself walking among the remnants of brokenness. And it will be important for you to walk through them without fear, or at least without letting fear overcome you. You will need to replace your fear with love and hope. The heavenly environment within you will need to be stronger than the earthly environment around you. Your love will need to be greater than your fear—or your discouragement or your concerns or your questions.

You will come to valleys full of dry bones. There is no way to avoid that. When Jesus talks about fields being ripe for the harvest, this is what He has in mind. This is where your harvest field is.

Maybe you were looking for the easiest and best harvest fields. But that is probably not where the Holy Spirit will take you.

It is not a very good idea to ask for the best harvest fields, not how natural minds define "best" anyway. From the Father's perspective, the best harvest fields are the most desperate. He wants

His ambassadors of love to prophesy the breath of hope and love into hopeless and loveless places. These valleys are where the greatest harvest is.

The reason for this is simple. Dark places do not have a darkness problem; they have a light problem. Hate-filled hearts do not have a hate problem; they have a love problem. Deadened hearts do not have a death problem; they have a life problem. Do you see where this is going?

God wants to use you—to put His words on your lips to prophesy His purposes. As you prophesy His words, the Holy Spirit—the breath of God, the wind—will release love and life. And He will do this in the places you might think are the most unlikely. After all, a valley of dry, lifeless bones seems to be a pretty unlikely center of revival. Deserts are unlikely places for tsunami waves of love. But these are exactly the places that need revivals and love.

This is where we see Jesus working in the Gospels.

Remember Zacchaeus? From the perspective of the people of Jericho, he was the least likely candidate to host Jesus in his home.

Remember that Samaritan village? From the disciples' perspective, it was good place to stop for water but an extremely unlikely field for revival.

What about the disciples themselves? Fishermen, a tax collector, a zealot—none of them were likely candidates to be world-changing love ambassadors.

There's a story of a man in the land beyond the Sea of Galilee—Gentile territory—who was possessed by a legion of demons. He was a very unlikely candidate for sparking a revival.

So can you guess who got saved in that region? The demoniac. And Jesus sent him back into his town to tell everyone what God had done.[1]

You will have a difficult time finding anything more unlikely than that. A man whose body had been possessed by the forces of hell was sent back into his town as a carrier of Heaven. He had been filled with twisted, distorted, deceptive thoughts and emotions, and suddenly he encountered Love in the flesh and became an ambassador of love himself.

You can track this theme all the way through the four Gospels and the Book of Acts, and you will see it everywhere. God chooses unlikely people to do unlikely things to spark unlikely revivals and movements. To put it another way, He loves the unlovable and calls the unloving to love the unlovable too.

If you have ever felt like an unlikely candidate to receive the Father's love, become the Father's love, and impart the Father's love, that's wonderful. You are right where you need to be. You are fully qualified to become a love ambassador.

Perhaps you feel powerless to move forward in that calling. Perfect. Ezekiel felt powerless surrounded by death and hopelessness too.

It can be very easy to feel powerless in modern society. To be honest, every one of us is powerless in our own strength, with our own love, and with access only to our own resources.

But this is not actually our position, is it? Nowhere does First Corinthians 13 tell us that the supernatural, perfect love of the heavenly family is weak and powerless. We are told that it is patient and kind and not self-serving. And we're told that it never fails. Many other beautiful adjectives are in there too. But "powerless" is not part of this kind of love.

In fact, our Papa's love is extraordinarily powerful. It releases the power of Heaven on earth. It is relentless, tenacious, and unquenchable. It will not be denied. It brings the justice of Heaven to every injustice on earth, the kindness of Heaven to every offense, the restoration of Heaven to every area of brokenness, wounding, and loss.

This is why fear is such a dangerous weapon against love. The thief wants us to feel powerless whenever we come up against the darkness and futility of this world. He wants our natural selves to submit to that environment. He wants us to remain blind to the security, assurance, and affirmation we have in the environment of Heaven, at rest in the heavenly family's love.

But as powerful as fear is, it must tremble in weakness in the face of love.

The reality is that we have been given all authority through the power of the Father's great love. We are completely secure, accepted, and adored. We walk in the authority of supernatural love.

Many of my most treasured memories and testimonies have come in valleys of dry bones. That morning I was awakened by a Muslim call to prayer and then sensed the Holy Spirit telling me to meet the imam I saw on TV led to a measure of fruitfulness I could not have imagined at the time.

That time of ministry in Cambodia among former Khmer Rouge led to testimonies that seemed very unlikely under the circumstances.

That time a stadium event got canceled but a visit to a wedding instead turned into a platform for a nationwide demonstration of the Father's love was not what I had envisioned.

In fact, God has reoriented my vision many times for me to see life in the midst of valleys of death. And He has had to remind me to see through the lenses of hope and love.

Once at a conference in Bangkok, I tried along with other leaders to listen to a speaker's message, but someone in the audience kept making disruptive noises. I wondered why the usher was not dealing with this problem and actually got a little irritated. My natural eyes saw what natural eyes normally see. But I was not looking through the right lenses.

The noise turned out to be a severely autistic boy, and his mother was helpless to quiet him.

"What do you think I see as a loving Father?" Papa asked me.

I suddenly realized that I had been more concerned about my own comfort level than about this woman and her son. That is a form of fear. This fear was trying to overcome love.

This boy had never been able to look into his mother's face or express his thoughts to her. She lived with that pain daily. She was trapped under the weight of broken hopes and dreams. I began to feel that weight too.

The mother brought her son up for prayer at the end of the meeting. My heart became filled with the Father's love for them. Several hundred people came forward for prayer, but I just sat there being filled with the Father's feelings.

So I was astonished when this boy pushed through the crowd and crawled up into my lap.

He grunted as if he wanted to say something. I could tell he was seeing something, hearing something, longing for something from God. We sat there for an hour and a half while people were receiving prayer. He and I were both soaking in the Father's love. Eventually he put his head on my chest. Something was definitely happening.

I do not know what actually happened in that moment, but something certainly happened that afternoon. When the mother came back for our evening service, she said her son had looked into her eyes for the first time and spoke his first words.

I wept for joy over what love had done for them.

I wept for what love had done for me.

And I wept for how distorted my vision had been at first.

But I realized how powerful it is to look in the face of Jesus and see the Father's love—and for people to look into our eyes and see Papa God's love made manifest in us.

This is how the Holy Spirit moves and breathes among us.

The Father created the world through the Son and the Spirit in love. The Son is the great revelation of this divine family's love. And the Holy Spirit is the implementer, the one who shapes our hearts with this perfect love, who gives us new eyes to see with and a new heart to feel with.

But none of that gets into our hearts if we are not stopping to ask the Holy Spirit what He thinks, sees, and feels. He is the mediator of the divine heartbeat. He has been poured into us so we can have the same heartbeat.

So we can look at a village of "those people" and have compassion.

So we can look at a disruptive boy and feel his mother's pain.

So we can notice in a terrifying moment that our fear is acting like it's stronger than our love, even when we know it is lying to us.

And so we can overcome that fear with the transforming power of supernatural love.

This is what the world needs from us—supernatural love carried by fearless hearts willing to serve as ambassadors of Heaven's perfect love wherever we go on earth.

Note

1. I encourage you to read the whole story. It's fascinating. You can find it in Mark 5:1–20.

CHAPTER 16

THE COMING LOVE REFORMATION

Once when I was visiting a key leader of a very strict form of Islam, I could tell he had been through much sadness and sorrow. I had been to his country before—when you go where I have gone over the last twenty-five years, you learn to build relationships and trust because that's what love does—and this imam and I always got together for dinner when I was in town.

But this time, my friend could not spend much time with me. His son had fallen and broken his neck while trying to put up some lights for a festival, and he had been in the hospital on a ventilator for several months. This father looked like a shadow of the man I remembered.

Three other people from my team were with me, and I asked if we could pray for this man's son. He looked at me a little strangely but said that would be okay. So with several imams standing there watching, I prayed in the name of Jesus that Papa God would touch this son and bring healing.

"Could I go to the hospital and pray for him?" I asked. Sometimes my faith level is a little bit higher in person than when I pray from a distance. He agreed, and eventually I ended up in this young man's hospital room while the rest of the team sat in the van with some armed guards.

I prayed several times. I had hoped we would see a miracle right then and there. My friend appreciated the prayers, but I could tell he might have thought they were a waste of time. But he was gracious. And I left saddened because nothing miraculous had happened.

I was leaving the next day for the capital city, and when I arrived, I felt a little depressed. I felt as if Papa God was asking me about it. "Leif, you seem disappointed."

"I am," I said. "Yesterday would have been an incredible opportunity for you to bring glory to Yourself." My friend was very influential and knew not only the prime minister of this country but also presidents, kings, and other leaders from all over the Arab world. A miracle would have made a very big impression on many influential people.

Then I heard the voice of Papa whispering. "Son, why do you still love with a hook? Why does there have to be an agenda?"

Then I heard a little voice whispering to me again. "Would you take your only son and trade places with this imam? Sacrificing your son as a quadriplegic in exchange for this imam's son being able to walk again?"

At first, I rebuked that voice as a word from satan.

But the words kept coming back, not as an audible voice but as a very strong inner voice. After about the fifth time, I knew it was God.

"Papa, I don't think I could do that. I don't know how to love that way."

I had been meditating on one verse for a long time in that season of my life—John 17:26, a prayer of Jesus. *"I have declared to them Your name, and will declare it, that the love with which You loved Me may be in them, and I in them."* Jesus prayed that the love of the Father would be in His followers just as He Himself was in them—not with an agenda, but just for the sake of experiencing and giving love. And not just any kind of love, but Papa God's kind of sacrificial love that always seeks the best for others.

I had been studying that verse, but that day, the verse was studying me. And I did not think I could love the way God loves.

I sat there in the lobby of my hotel and began to weep.

In the next moment, I could feel something like honey, that liquid love that flows when we are having an encounter with the Father's love. I was so overwhelmed. This love of God would give up an only begotten Son—to leave Heaven and come to earth, to become shame, to become sin, to become love that we can see. I kept feeling waves and waves of this love coming over me again. I will never forget it.

Then the voice said one more thing: "What you are experiencing now is like a glass compared to the ocean of love I am about to pour out."

A few minutes later, my in-country coordinator came into the lobby and told me that the imam was on the phone asking for me. He wanted to know where I was. My coordinator told him I was right there with him in the capital city.

"No, he is not," the imam said. "I just saw him. He visited me in my headquarters and told me he was going to the hospital.

Then the hospital called and said my son was getting off the ventilator and was starting to move."

A creative miracle was taking place, apparently while I was in a hospital many miles away from where I was actually sitting in the flesh.

I realized that the words Papa God had spoken to me a few moments before—that the love I was experiencing was only a small glass compared to the ocean of love He was planning to pour out—was an invitation for this generation. I believe we are about to enter into a new reformation.

An Agape Reformation

I mentioned the idea of a love reformation in the introduction to this book, and I believe it is more than just a movement that is coming. I am expecting something on the scale of a great reformation like we have had in the past—something that changes the character of Christianity from the way many believers have been experiencing it.

The Protestant Reformation restored the foundation of grace as the central aspect of salvation. It was a very doctrinal and theological reformation, but it changed the way many people understand salvation and brought it back in line with New Testament Christianity.

We also experienced a reformation in the last century that focused on the work of the Holy Spirit. It restored the importance of God's power in our experience, also to bring us back in line with New Testament faith.

So we have had a grace reformation and a power reformation. But the next reformation is about love.

Most Christians throughout history have understood that love is a vital part of the Gospel. This is very plain in Scripture. But I cannot think of any generation of Christians for the last two thousand years that has lived out this message of love the way God has intended. Rarely have believers made it their priority to bring the love of Heaven down to earth so people can experience the environment of the perfect family from before time. We have not made our world feel like the Father's living room.

Now is the time. In fact, I believe this is one reason that we are seeing so much hatred and polarization in our world right now. The enemy is sowing opposite seeds in the world, like he has done even from the beginning. He senses that this message is about to be revealed. He wants to divide because love will bring unity. And tsunami waves of love are coming soon.

We are seeing some signs of this love reformation in many places around the world, even if they are not very visible to many people yet. Papa God is inviting His people to encounter His love, live from a whole heart, and walk in the power that supernatural love brings.

This will mean pursuing His love, asking for and preparing for encounters, and stewarding the seeds of love faithfully. But when Papa God's children are immersed in His love and allow it to touch and heal the deepest areas of their lives, the seeds of reformation have been planted.

I could tell you many examples of this. Agape love has always worked powerfully in the world.

Paul and Ahlmira, whom you met in chapter 6, have seen world-changing love in their ministry—their family of believers. One woman named Mira, who had been part of their church in the Philippines in her college days, returned years later with her husband and a high school–aged daughter. Ahlmira told her, "You are home," and it hit Mira like a *rhema* word from God for the moment. She embraced the family atmosphere.

Then she extended the family atmosphere to many others, especially the women she was discipling in her ministry group. She made it feel like Papa God's living room. The group grew in love and started noticing anyone God would highlight to them.

Mira traveled more than an hour to visit the mother of one of her group's members, and the mother was so touched and felt so valued that she invited them to start a gathering in her town to help kids in the area.

Every month they would gather, first with a few children, then with twenty or thirty, with many of them bringing their mothers with them. Mira's group would teach Bible lessons, provide some food, and pray for the sick. People were healed. Love overflowed with acts of kindness and generosity, and power flowed with it.

When one of Mira's group member's sisters was jailed for drug use, the group began visiting her and bringing her food. This gathering grew too—many other inmates got to hear testimonies and Bible teachings. The warden eventually asked Mira to formalize their work as a recognized jail ministry and help conduct some programs for inmates. Some inmates who have since been released have joined Bible study groups and spread love to their communities.

What Mira received, she gave. And what others received from her, they gave. And the waves of love continue, transforming lives, families, neighborhoods, communities, and even distant places.

About an hour away from Mira, a woman named Cynthia leads a community outreach in a fishing village on a large lake. The outreach had begun with a marriage course that restored marriages and helped turn drinking, womanizing fishermen—not uncommon in that community—into loving husbands and devoted community servants.

Cynthia and her co-leaders continued to minister to that village after the marriage course was over, leading Bible studies, prayer gatherings, and compassion ministries.

One day, a fisherman named Elmer, who had recently attended an event hosted by Paul's church, prayed to have a bigger catch. God answered him miraculously. Instead of the normal daily catch of about forty-five pounds, Elmer had to call other fishermen to help him haul more than three thousand pounds into five boats. This amazing blessing made quite a stir in that community.

With the outreach's assistance, a young woman in that village became the first student to pass the college entrance test and be able to attend. She did so well that she was also awarded a scholarship—the only person in her larger municipality to receive one.

Cynthia had come from a poor family herself and had graduated college because of God's grace. Love has made her passionate about helping poor people in this village to rise up from poverty and be transformed. Her work has even become a model for the local government. Supernatural love brings restoration.

We saw very early in this book that love looks for manifestations. It seeks ways to bring others in. It longs to be expressed. The perfect love of the divine family pours into Papa God's family gatherings in this world. It moves out in order to draw others in. It creates a little bit of Heaven on earth.

These kinds of testimonies are occurring all over the world. When the love of the perfect family comes to earth, lives change.

Love 2.0

A few years ago, I led our ministry's Kingdom Family Gathering in Penang, Malaysia. While we were in worship one day, I started to feel overwhelmed. I could feel my spirit being lifted up.

I have only had three experiences like this in my life, and this one was a little different from the others. It was almost like I was being lifted above the room. My body was standing on the floor, but my spirit could look down and see the room.

In the next moment, I could look down and see the world. I would see a country, and it would be like I was suddenly there. Then I would think about a different country, and I was immediately there. I could feel the love of God for this world—waves and waves of it—and it was overwhelming.

When my spirit finally came back to my body, I could not minister. I was supposed to start ministering, but people had to carry me. I was undone for hours after this encounter.

During that time, God spoke, "Leif, I need you to be able to stand and minister in My glory. There are some cracks in your foundation, so I wanted you to experience more of My glory. But you could not handle it. You were crushed when the weight of My glory came in."

And then He said, "You have loved Me well, and you have loved the world well. But you have not loved you the way that I have loved you."

And Papa's love began coming into those cracks. It was the greatest experience with love that I have had since my baptism of love more than two decades ago.

I knew at that moment that God was preparing a tsunami wave of love to wash over the world. He loves this world, and a mass repentance is coming. When my spirit was high above looking across the world, I could go into places and feel the pain of what was going on. It was such an overwhelming experience that I could not handle it. There were times when I felt that I was going to die, and I had to pull myself back because of the weight of it. But I know God was showing me some of the things that are to come.

This has been confirmed several times by prophetic words and ministry experiences. The first time I met a certain prophet who is pretty well known, he told me he could see a wave, like a baptism of love 2.0. He did not know I had already written a book called *Baptism of Love*, but he was seeing an upgrade of what God wants to do in covering the world with His love.

I knew I was being invited into a new encounter. This would not be a supernatural love encounter like before. That had come to fill a deficiency of love. A love deficiency is a God deficiency, and when His glory comes in, there is no God deficiency at all. He is there, so love is there in glory.

This would be an upgrade of what is already there. And I believe many people are being given that same invitation into a new encounter with the Father's love.

You probably can guess where all of this begins. It starts with a seed of love that becomes a tree of love that becomes a forest of love. It starts with a trickle that becomes a river that becomes an ocean of love and glory that covers the earth.

It begins with how the Father loves you.

When God spoke to me in that experience in Penang and told me that I had not loved me the way He had loved me, it made me think about how Jesus knew the Father's love even before His ministry began.

Have you experienced the same love from the Father that Jesus experienced from the Father?

He was so well loved that He did not have to prove anything any longer.

He was so well loved that He could live in freedom and set other people free.

He was so well loved that even in the middle of His most difficult tests and opposition He knew whose He was.

This is the power that begins the agape reformation that will cover the earth with the Father's glory.

You need to be overwhelmed by His love. Then when you have received His love, you can become love and release love.

And as you do, lives will be changed. Communities will see what God is like. Broken lives and relationships will be healed. Divisions will be bridged.

And glory will cover the earth a little bit more each day.

CHAPTER 17

LOVE'S HUMBLE AND GLORIOUS MISSION

Let's look back over the course of history, and even further back into the family before time, and see where we have been.

Our template for love is found in the eternal relationships of the divine family, the three-in-one God living in perfect fellowship as Father, Son, and Spirit.

This love is the driving force behind creation and all its beauty. Love always longs to be shared, so the Father, Son, and Spirit made this world—with many deeply personal and artistic touches—and placed within it a being with the same capacity to give and receive love. *"Let **Us** make man in Our image,"* God said (Genesis 1:26). And He did, breathing the life and love of the divine family into humanity.

The first family on earth stepped out of that love and, in that process, developed orphan hearts that no longer trusted their

Father's heart or received the extravagant love He wanted them to receive.

And as we have seen, the phenomenon of the orphan heart has had many catastrophic outcomes in our world.

Now let's pause for a moment and be very clear about something. I don't know if you have noticed this, but love is not mentioned at all in the first three chapters of Genesis.

You will not find it anywhere in there. If you had never seen a Bible before and picked one up and started reading at the beginning, you wouldn't necessarily know that love was the driving force behind this world. We have to read the rest of Scripture to see what was really going on there.

But when we do, it lights up the story. A veil is removed from our eyes so we can see that the love that existed before the foundation of the world is actually the reason for the foundation of the world. Love *is* the foundation.

For if God is love, and if God made human beings in His likeness, then we are made in the image of love. And if we are made in the image of love, it should be very clear that we were made in order to be loved and to love—to give and receive the same kind of love that motivated God to create us in the first place. Because if God breathed life into the dust He had formed to create a man, He breathed something of Himself. And it would be impossible to breathe something of Himself that was not thoroughly characterized by love.

Here is the very important point: we came into existence as a love-saturated creation and are being restored back into that same love-saturated purpose—a new creation that includes a new Heaven and earth filled with people who have been given a new breath from their Father.

That's what the story line of Scripture shows us, isn't it?

Human beings acted unlovingly and self-centeredly for a very long time—Cain killing Abel; a flood that destroyed most of humanity because of its wickedness; a tower reaching into the Heavens so human beings could make a name for themselves, their orphan hearts reaching out for some kind of meaning and identity.

And along the way there are glimpses of love being woven even into this dreadful start—Abel's pleasing offering, Enoch walking closely with God, Noah's family being preserved so the thread of love could continue.

And eventually, God established His covenant of love and faith with Abraham and his descendants. He chose Israel as His beloved people, the apple of His eye.[1] He revealed His glory and love to Moses and established a covenant that many prophets and rabbis would interpret as a marriage contract and a betrothal ceremony.

Don't think too little of that picture. It's huge. It is implied in the words of many prophets, and it is plainly written in the words of Jeremiah: *"I remember you, the kindness of your youth, the love of your betrothal, when you went after Me in the wilderness, in a land not sown"* (Jeremiah 2:2).

This is part of a love poem from God to His people. And there are lots of love poems like that in the Bible.

The Song of Songs is a long one, and a very intimate one too. It reads on a personal level, to be sure; on the surface, it's clearly about human romance and intimacy. But it is often interpreted by Jewish and Christian commentators as an allegory of the love between God and His people. The Love before time is intensely and passionately expressed to human beings who are becoming love in the flesh through the covenant of love we have been given.

The rest of the prophets bear testimony to this. God's words through them are not just about doing the right thing. His message is about faithfulness—the kind of faithfulness you expect to find in a marriage. This is why idolatry in the Old Testament is not just described as unfaithfulness. It is portrayed as adultery. No one uses words like that unless they are speaking the language of love.

The Gospels show us many examples of Love in the flesh— the incarnation, Jesus the Son as an expression of the perfect family's love. And it calls us to become love in the flesh ourselves, filled with the Spirit of love as followers of the Son of love.

This Son of love often referred to Himself as "the bridegroom," by the way. He pointed to the end of this story as a wedding banquet and portrayed Himself as the Son who is looking for a bride.[2] This is the picture we are supposed to look forward to, and it's all about love.

This is where we are now—in the middle of the story of God covering the earth with His glory, which is characterized by His love. We participate in this mission because the only way knowledge of the glory/love of God will cover the earth as waters cover the sea (see Habakkuk 2:14) is through the people who carry God's love and glory in them, just as Jesus prayed:

> *The glory which You gave Me I have given them, that*
> *they may be one just as We are one: I in them, and You in*
> *Me; that they may be made perfect in one, and that the*

world may know that You have sent Me, and have loved them as You have loved Me (John 17:22–23).

We are very important parts of this plan.

Now that we've looked back over this story, let's look ahead to the end of it. The only way to really understand the beginning of a story is to see its conclusion because the beginning and end work together to interpret the whole meaning.

And what do we see at the end? A wedding. The marriage of the Lamb of God, the sacrificial offering of God, a symbol of the kind of selfless love that transcends time and all other conditions.

The bride has made herself ready for the bridegroom. (See Revelation 19:7.)

The holy city comes down from Heaven to earth like a beautiful bride walking the aisle. (See Revelation 21:2.)

The Spirit and the bride speak as one—*"Come!"* they say—to invite others into this love (Revelation 22:17).

And if we had wondered at all if this magnificent cosmic wedding was supposed to serve as a conclusion to the story that began way back in Genesis at the foundation of the world, we are given some very big hints.

There's a river of life flowing from the throne of God, just like a river flowed from Eden. (See Genesis 2:10; Revelation 22:1.)

The tree of life that human beings had once been driven away from—in love, remember—is rooted on each side of that river in the holy city. (See Genesis 3:22–24; Revelation 22:2.)

And the leaves of that tree are given for the healing of the nations. (See Revelation 22:2–4.) No more curse. No more futility. No more pain. No more skewed perspectives, unhealthy agendas, or searching for significance or affirmation or acceptance.

No more orphan heart!

Because just like at the beginning, when the Father breathed life and love into the face of the first man, and the first man gazed back into the face of his loving Father, those who serve God in love and faithfulness are given the most intimate gift they could possibly receive: *"They shall see His face"* (Revelation 22:4).

Hearts are healed. The nations find their purpose. The families from which those nations came are families once again. Just like the family whose love called all of this into being.

The thread of love has pulled the whole cloth back together, tied up its loose ends, and made it beautiful.

The Picture of Our Family's Love

The night before His crucifixion, Jesus had a meal with His disciples. When John wrote about this gathering, he began it with a profound statement: *"Having loved His own who were in the world, He loved them to the end"* (John 13:1).

Of course this is what Jesus did. Love before time doesn't waver, doesn't expire, and doesn't fade away. It cannot be thwarted or overcome. It began outside of time, so it is not limited by anything within time. It endures to the end.

Then Jesus demonstrated what it means to love. He poured water into a bowl, took off His outer garment, grabbed a towel like a servant would do, and began to wash His friends' feet.[3] Why? Because this is what love looks like.

Peter was not sure this was acceptable. He objected. Jesus explained that it had to be this way. You cannot give love unless you have received love. So Peter sat back and received love.

After Jesus washed all the disciples' feet, He got up, put His normal garments back on, and sat down. (See John 13:2–12.) That's a beautiful picture of Love in the flesh, the perfect love of the heavenly family taking on human form and serving in love.

Paul pictured that same trajectory of love and humility in his letter to the Philippians:

> [Jesus] *made Himself of no reputation, taking the form of a bondservant, and coming in the likeness of men. And being found in appearance as a man, He humbled Himself and became obedient to the point of death, even the death of the cross. Therefore God also has highly exalted Him and given Him the name which is above every name* (Philippians 2:7–9).

As Jesus did when He washed the disciples' feet, He set aside His divine nature (His heavenly garments), took the form of a servant (picking up a bowl and towel), humbled Himself (by washing dirty feet), and became obedient even to death. Then God reclothed Him in honor (putting His heavenly clothes back on), exalted Him above every name, and seated Him on Heaven's throne.[4]

But Jesus did not stop with this act of service and love. He went on to teach His friends to do the same kind of things for one another.

The Lord and Lover, the King, the Son of the Father, Love in the flesh showed the way.

And then, beautifully, remarkably, He sat down with them for a meal, like a family where love, acceptance, affirmation, and fellowship flourish.

This is an intimate setting. If you aren't sure about that, look at John's posture as this family of friends ate together. He leaned against Jesus and listened to His secret words. (See John 13:23–25.) And later, when he wrote this Gospel, he kept referring to himself as the disciple whom Jesus loved.

During this evening together, Jesus taught these friends all about love. This is when He urged them to love one another as He had loved them, which in turn was how the Father had loved the Son. (See John 15:9–10.)

It's when He told them that the world would know them by their love. (See John 13:35.)

It's when He explained that those who love Him would keep His word, and the Father and Son and Spirit—the entire heavenly family—would come and make Their home with them. (See John 14:23–26.)

And this is when, just a few hours later, He would pray that amazing prayer about sharing His glory with His friends so that the world would know His love, their love, and therefore the Father's love, and that the love of the Father and the Son—that perfect, supernatural, love before time—would be in those who have loved Him. (See John 17:20–26.)

Wow. That scarlet thread of love woven throughout Scripture and history led to this climactic moment.

The whole purpose of creation was being fulfilled.

The people who would soon be filled with the Spirit/breath/wind/glory/love of God were getting a very profound taste of it.

The movement to cover the earth with the glorious love of the Father, just as the waters cover the sea, was being launched.

And soon, Love in the flesh breathed the Spirit of love into these followers just as the Spirit of love had hovered over the waters way back at the beginning and breathed life into the first human being.

And as He did, He gave them that mission statement we noticed earlier: *"As the Father has sent Me, I also send you"* (John 20:21).

To paraphrase this a little, in the very same way the Father sent the Son—in that Spirit of love, imparting love to human beings, turning them into love in the flesh just as the Son had become Love in the flesh—the Son was now sending out His beloved.

Above all our evangelistic efforts, above all signs and wonders, above all our Kingdom influence in all the spheres of society, this is our calling.

I remember lying on the floor several years ago and soaking in the Father's love. I was so tired and burdened. It was one of those seasons when the journey was costly and painful.

As I lay there, I sensed Jesus saying, "I'm going to wash your feet."

I was like Peter. "No, Lord. I can't do this."

But like He said to Peter, Jesus said, "Yes." I had to receive in order to be able to give. And having already given much, I had to receive more.

So I took off my shoes and socks, lay on a mat on the floor, and literally began to feel someone massaging my feet. I wept and wept. I knew the King of kings and Lord of lords had come and washed my feet, just as He had done with His disciples, just as He does with anyone whose heart belongs to Him.

I got up healed and refreshed. And I knew the words Jesus was saying to me, which were the same words He spoke to His disciples. He wanted me to love in the same way He loves me, to continue in the love that I had been shown. He wants that for all of us.

In our relationship with Jesus, we have unveiled faces. We are free to experience love and glory. This is part of our journey.

And it is a necessary part. We cannot see transformation in the world until we see transformation in our hearts. We have nothing to offer orphan hearts until we know the perfect love and acceptance the Father has given us in adopting us into His family.

Good works, diligent study, compelling arguments, and strong relationships aren't enough by themselves. They are good, but we need personal face-to-face encounters with the Father and the love that carries us through our journeys between those encounters. With our spiritual eyes, we need to see the love in His eyes, feel the affection of His heart, study His ways, and build relationships with others from this place of heavenly love. We need to live from love rather than strive for it.

We have been adopted into the family of love. We have been welcomed into the warmth and acceptance of the Father's living room. We have seen Love in the flesh and received the Spirit of love He gave us.

It's a heavenly encounter on earth, and an earthly process that carries us to heavenly places.

We have been, are being, and will continue to be baptized in love.

Notes

1   That's how Zechariah 2:8 describes Israel even after a long season of exile that they had brought upon themselves due to their own lack of love for their Father.

2. Jesus pictured Himself as Bridegroom in Matthew 9:15; 22:1–14; 25:1–13; Mark 2:18–20; Luke 5:33–35; and John 3:29.

3. He even washed the feet of a friend who was about to betray Him and another who was about to deny Him. He knew that, but He loved them anyway because that's what supernatural, perfect, unconditional love does.

4. The whole passage, Philippians 2:5–11, parallels this act of humility and love as John presents it in chapter 13 of his Gospel.

REFLECTING ON SECTION 3

Questions to Think and Pray Through

- What is the relationship between your private moments of encounter and God's glory covering the earth? How can your private moments lead to transformation in the world? Why do you think He has arranged the world so that our intimacy with Him does not always remain private?

- What is the difference between a visitation from God and a habitation of Him? What benefits does a habitation of love have that a visitation does not?

- Do you agree with the spiritual principle that you only have authority over what you love? Why or why not? How can this principle shape how you pray and relate to other people?

- How does knowing your own new identity change your view of other people? How do ambassadors of love think differently from other people— especially with regard to dark places, difficult cases, crisis moments, and fear?

- In what ways have you observed believers trying to change the world through debates about theology and public policy? As important as these can be, why is love so much more powerful? In what ways does it represent the nature of God?

- Have there been times when you have loved with a "hook" or an agenda? How does perfect, supernatural love help us overcome that tendency?

Envisioning Exercise

Frequently and confidently envision tsunamis of love flooding over your family, neighborhood, workplace, church, community, city, nation, and world—even the darkest places. Practice seeing yourself as part of those waves, sent out on a mission to demonstrate love wherever it is needed.

Prayer

Ask Papa God how He wants to send you out as a love ambassador. Pray for His love to fill any cracks in your foundation and for Him to supernaturally empower you to know the width, length, depth, and height of His love. Ask Him to put specific people and situations on your heart and to give you wisdom and power as you enter into those lives and situations in love.

Next Steps

Think of a difficult situation or relationship that affects you today. Ask, "What does love look like in this situation?" As you pray through this situation, listen for insights that might help you apply love and take practical steps to show it. Memorize and meditate on Luke 19:10 as a mission statement of what love is sent into this world to do.

THE SUM OF IT ALL

It's not surprising that the verse that best summarizes the entire Bible is one that emphasizes the Father's love.

God loved the world so much that He gave His only Son for it. (See John 3:16.) He sent His Son into the world not to judge the world but to love it back into the family.

This verse captures the motivation of the Father.

It assures us that the world is not one of those hard cases that can't be reached.

It tells us that we ought to love the world too. After all, if this is the Father's heart, and the Son sends us in the same way the Father sent Him, and the Father puts His Spirit into us, then loving the world is right at the center of God's purpose for our lives.

It reminds us that we can't love as selectively as our natural hearts want to.

God loves not just the Christians and Jews but the Hindus, Buddhists, Muslims, atheists, and every other flavor of religious people we come across. He loves Democrats and Republicans. He loves hypocrites and vagrants, criminals and the self-righteous, the rich and the poor, the young and the old, prisoners, people with personality disorders, people who love Him back and people who don't.

He loves all of these people so much that He sent what was most valuable to Him—a member of the heavenly family who lived in perfect fellowship with Him—to be sacrificed.

He created this world for intimate love with this family, and He paid an enormous price to restore it to this intimate love.

And those who have been restored in this intimate love are sent out to impart it to others and bring them into it, to cover the earth as the waters cover the sea.

ABOUT LEIF HETLAND

LEIF HETLAND is founder and president of Global Mission Awareness. He ministers globally bringing an impartation of God's love, healing, and apostolic authority through a paradigm of kingdom family. A forerunner in modern-day missions, Leif has brought the gospel into the most spiritually dark areas of the world. Over one million souls have been saved through his ministry.

He has written numerous books, including his bestsellers *Seeing Through Heaven's Eyes, Giant Slayers* and *Healing the Orphan Spirit.*